Terrifying Tec

For Guitar

Carl Culpepper says, "Gee...Thanx!" to the following
for their help and support on this project and others:
God, Judy Smith, Johnny 'V' & Jimmy Atkinson, "Skeetz" Frasier, 'Colonel' Gary F. Montgomery,
all at HLC, David Bergstrom & Ovation Guitars, Staff & Students of the Atlanta Institute of Music,
George Petsch and the Atlanta Guitar Center, Randy Hoexter, Sid Woolfolk, and everyone who buys this product.

ISBN 0-7935-5164-1

HAL•LEONARD®
CORPORATION
7777 W. BLUEMOUND RD. P.O. BOX 13819 MILWAUKEE, WI 53213

Visit Hal Leonard on the internet at http://www.halleonard.com

PREFACE

Technical facility is an important component of solid musicianship, regardless of musical style. Along with inspiration and a good ear, your physical ability to play is what gets the music from inside your head to the instrument. Limited technique could easily limit your realization of the music you envision. On the other hand, technical versatility can very well inspire you to create more freely, without the fear of the inability to follow through.

The purpose of this book is to help you, the guitarist, to overcome physical barriers with a wide variety of exercises, as well as enlighten you to methods that will expedite progress. By the same token, this is certainly not an attempt to unearth every possible melodic sequence. By taking a thorough approach with each series of exercises presented here, you will develop a solid platform of technical facility and practice habits from which to pursue a vast universe of creative guitar music.

Since the primary focus of this book is the development of techniques, the subject of music theory is not explained in any depth. However, some reference to melodic and rhythmic devices is made in the explanation of the examples. The scale and arpeggio appendix located at the end of the book will be helpful to those who haven't previously studied these fingerings. While the standard notation will reveal rhythmic detail to those who read music, the performances of the examples on the accompanying sound recording will thoroughly demonstrate rhythmic characteristics to those learning from the tablature.

PRACTICE TIPS

The development of good guitar technique requires patience, persistence, and attention to detail. Don't take on too much at once. Try adding just a few exercises to your daily practice routine, giving yourself time to refine them before moving on. Skipping ahead or moving on too soon may result in the reinforcement of bad habits or even cause burn-out when it suddenly seems too difficult. Likewise, "skimming" a large amount of exercises is simply a waste of time. There are no short cuts. By patiently working with a smaller amount of material, your progress will be much more obvious and rewarding.

When tackling each exercise, start slowly, paying close attention to all of the details important to its performance. Establishing good habits from the start is far easier than "reprogramming" later. Once you become comfortable with the exercise and can consistently reproduce it without mistakes, gradually raise your tempo.

I strongly suggest the use of a metronome for this procedure. The mechanized pulse is indispensable in solidifying your performance of the exercises rhythmically. The metronome also provides a gauge with which you can measure your progress as you gradually increase the tempo on an exercise.

In regard to electric guitarists who use effects (distortion/overdrive, delay, compression, chorus, etc.) be sure to practice the exercises in this book with dry, clean tone (no effects) at first. This will reveal any less obvious mistakes and weaknesses in general execution. Once you are able to perform an exercise using dry and clean tone, add your usual effects in order to further refine your technique and ultimately achieve the desired tone.

WARNING: Never practice to the point of pain. This can cause injury to the fragile muscles and tendons of the hands and wrist. If you experience any discomfort, stop and rest your hands. Begin practicing again, only when you feel 100%.

* ❷ Tuning Notes

ALTERNATE PICKING

Basic Concepts

Alternate picking is one of the most important techniques for any guitarist who uses the pick (or plectrum). The basic idea of alternate picking involves steady alternation of downstrokes and upstrokes. Most guitarists are familiar with this concept to some degree. However, breaking the technique down to its most basic elements can help you master it systematically.

The wide physical motion of chord strumming will clearly demonstrate the details of the pick strokes. In Example 1A, notice that you make a "silent upstroke" between each set of quarter notes in order to prepare for the next downstroke. By simply striking the chord on the upstroke, you can produce eighth notes with no extra effort (Example 1B).

❸ Examples 1-16

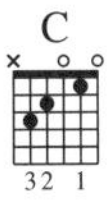

⊓ = downstroke. V = upstroke.

Example 1A **Example 1B**

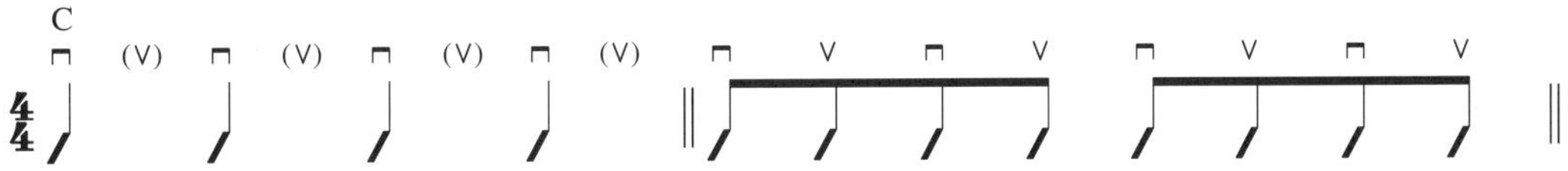

Let's try mixing quarter notes and eighth notes.

Example 2

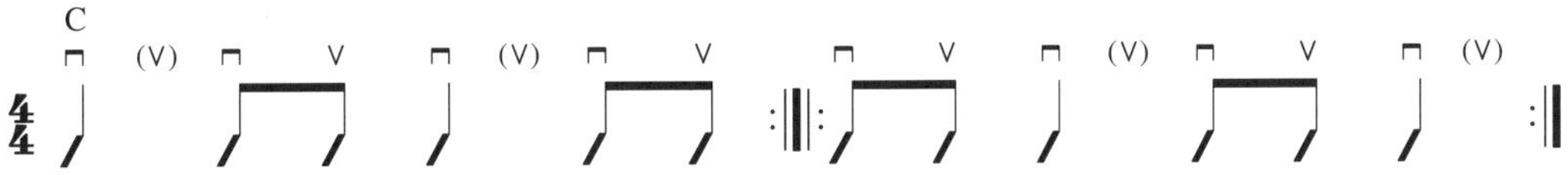

Alternate picking is just as easily applied to syncopated rhythms. Notice that the downstroke is occasionally silent as you keep the steady eighth-note alternation.

Example 3

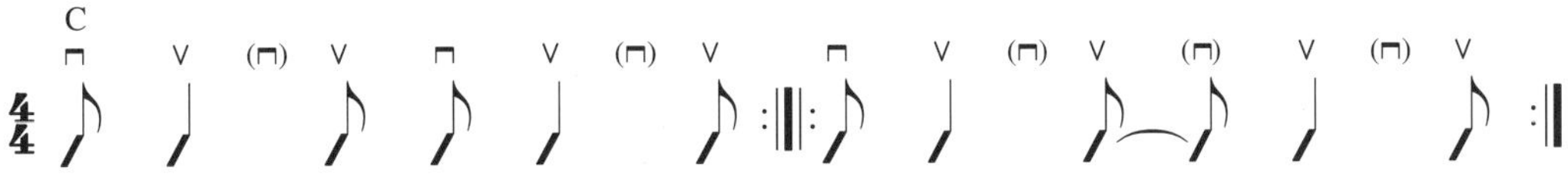

* represents CD track number.

If we play steady eighth notes with downstrokes you will see that all the previously mentioned principles apply when making the transition to sixteenth notes.

Example 4

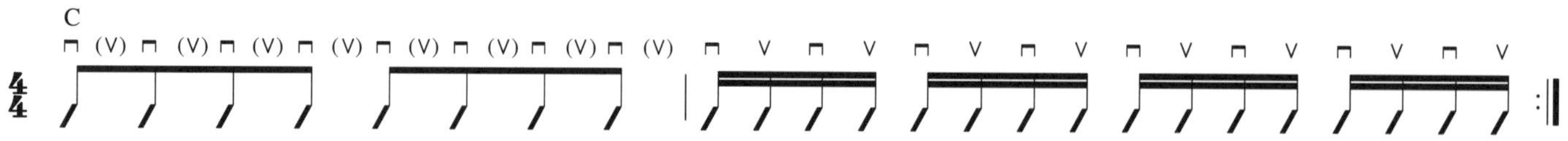

Let's mix eighth and sixteenth notes.

Example 5

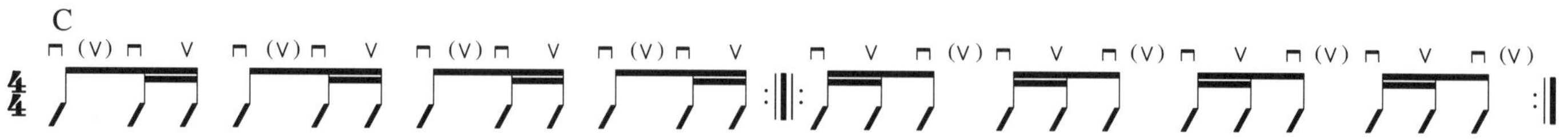

Compare the syncopated rhythms in this example to the ones in Example 3. Play this example as slowly as you need to in order to fully comprehend the motion of the right hand.

Example 6

The next step in understanding the basic concepts of alternate picking is the application of these principles to a single string. Notice that the difference in execution of the quarter and eighth notes in the following example and the strumming in Examples 1-3 is simply a refinement of right hand motion.

Example 7

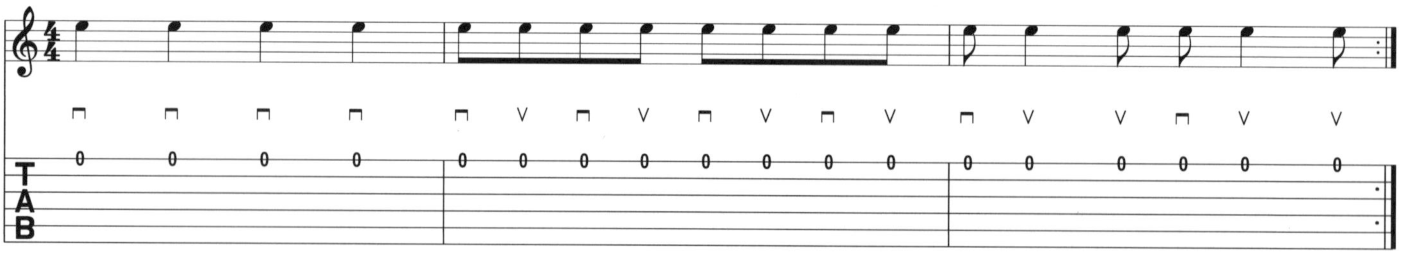

Examples 8, 9, and 10 employ the same rhythms as examples 4, 5, and 6, respectively, using single notes as opposed to chords.

Example 8

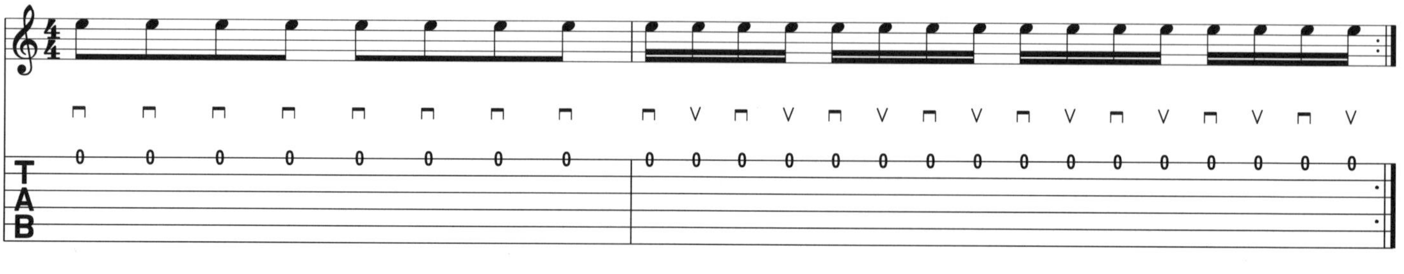

Example 9

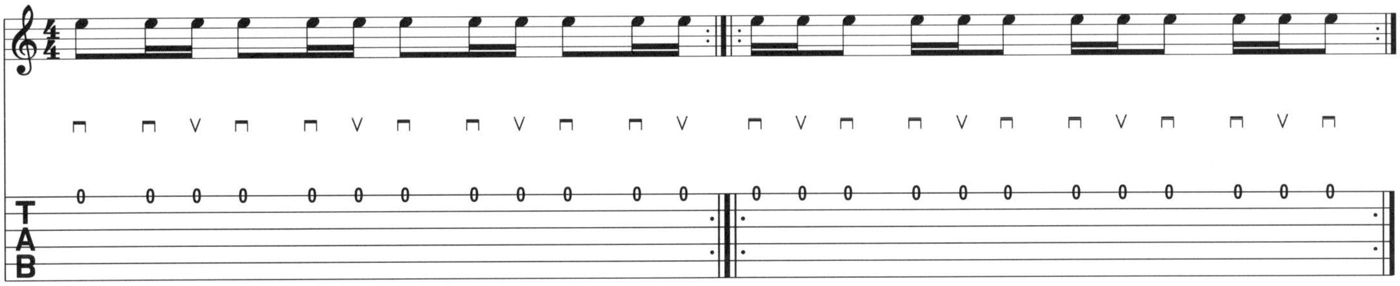

Example 10

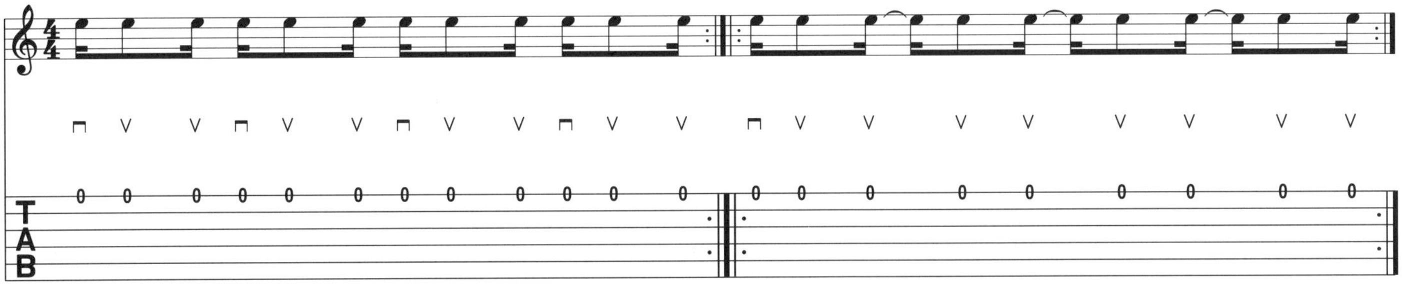

Let's apply alternate picking using an eighth-note rhythm to a one octave C scale. Take care to keep the pick stroke in order (downstroke on each down-beat, upstroke on each up-beat).

Example 11

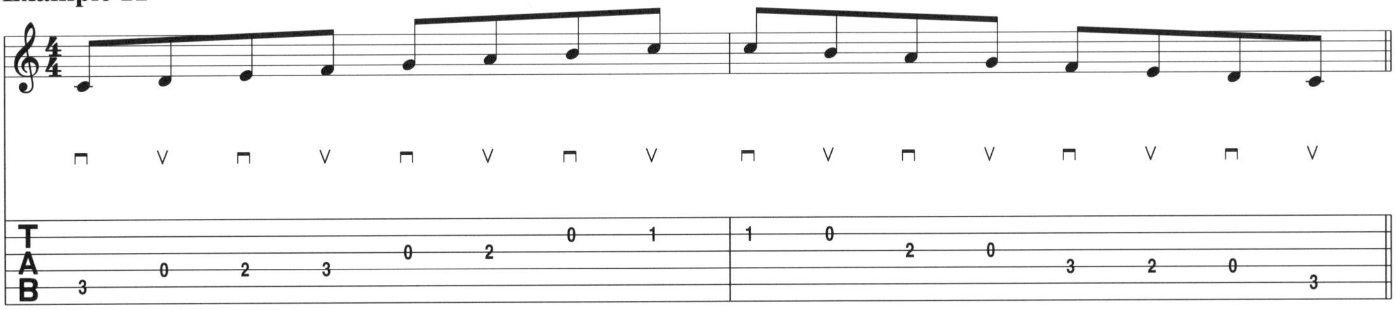

We'll use the same scale for the sixteenth-note rhythm in this example. Notice that, even though the notes are the same as Example 11, it is easier to lose the steady alternation and play two successive pick strokes in the same direction. Play as slowly as necessary to achieve perfection.

Example 12

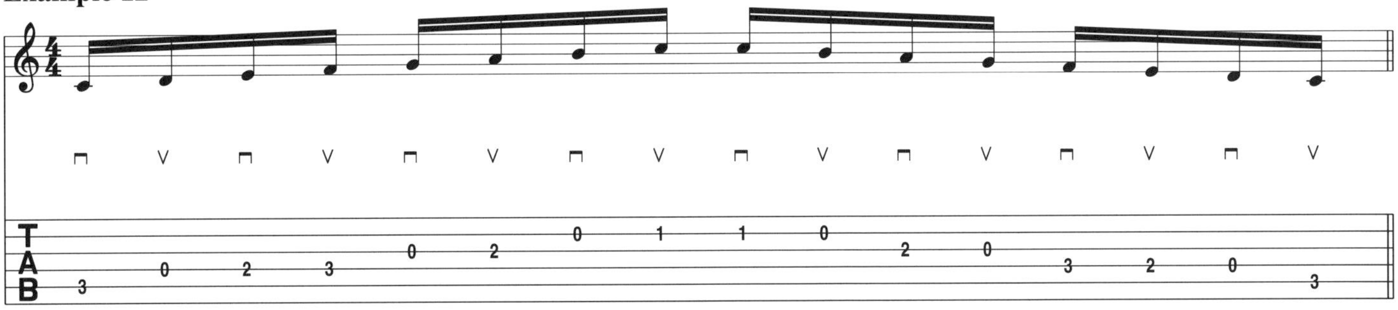

Take a close look at the down-up-down, up-down-up sequence that occurs when alternate picking is applied to steady eighth-note triplets in this example.

Example 13

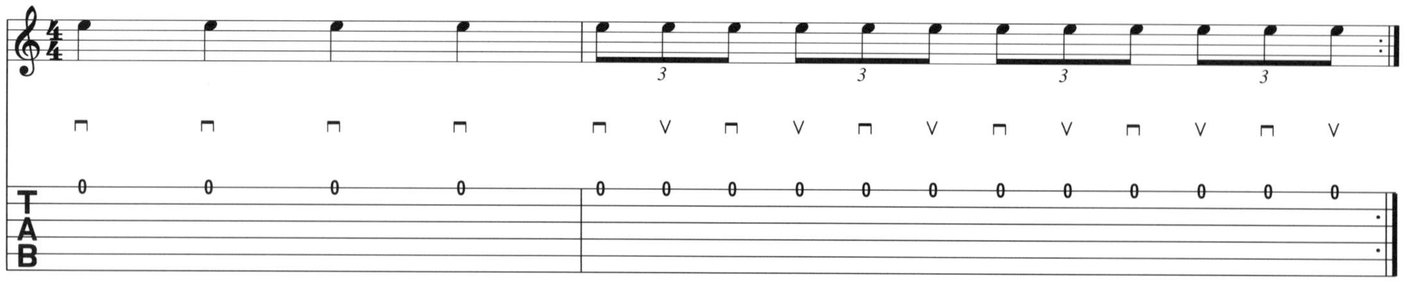

When mixing quarter- and eighth-note triplets, it is usually best to stick with strict alternation rather than the "silent pickstrokes" shown in earlier examples.

Example 14

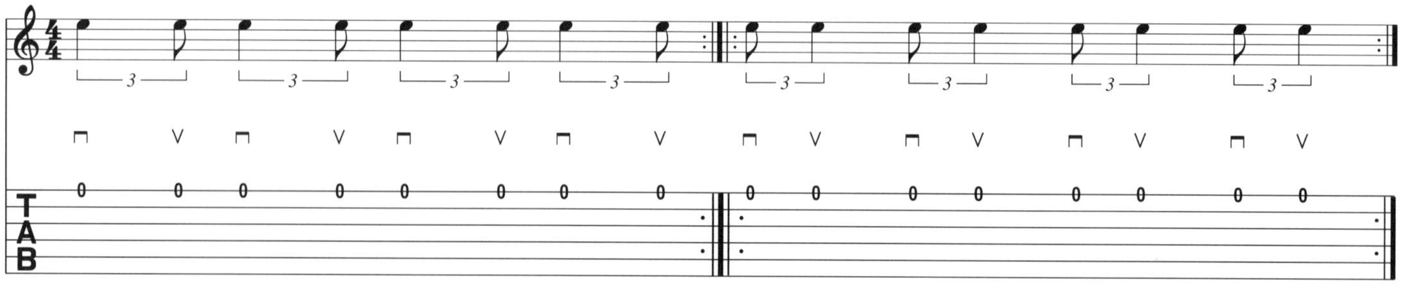

Let's apply steady eighth-note triplets to the one octave C scale. Take special care to use alternation consistently.

Example 15

Use strict alternation for mixed triplets.

Example 16

Symmetrical and Chromatic Exercises

Symmetrical and chromatic exercises can be quite helpful in the development of speed and synchronization with alternate picking. With the left hand's job simplified to repetitive shapes, your mind is free to concentrate on right hand mechanics.

Each of the following symmetrical and chromatic examples should be moved up chromatically (one fret at a time) to the twelfth position and back down for a complete workout.

The following example utilizes a two note per string pattern. Take note of the optional left hand fingering.

4 Examples 17-25

Example 17

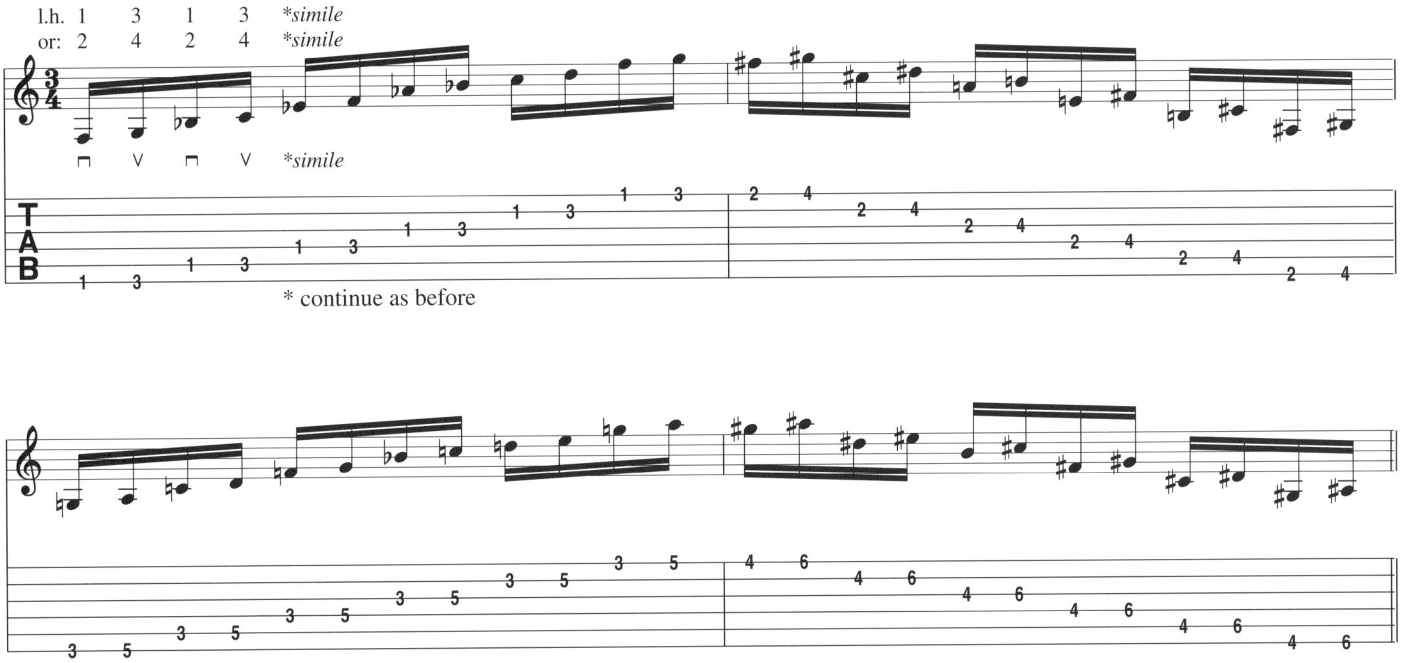

Here, we'll simply turn the sequence around.

Example 18

Here, the sequences ascend and descend in alternative fashion.

Example 19

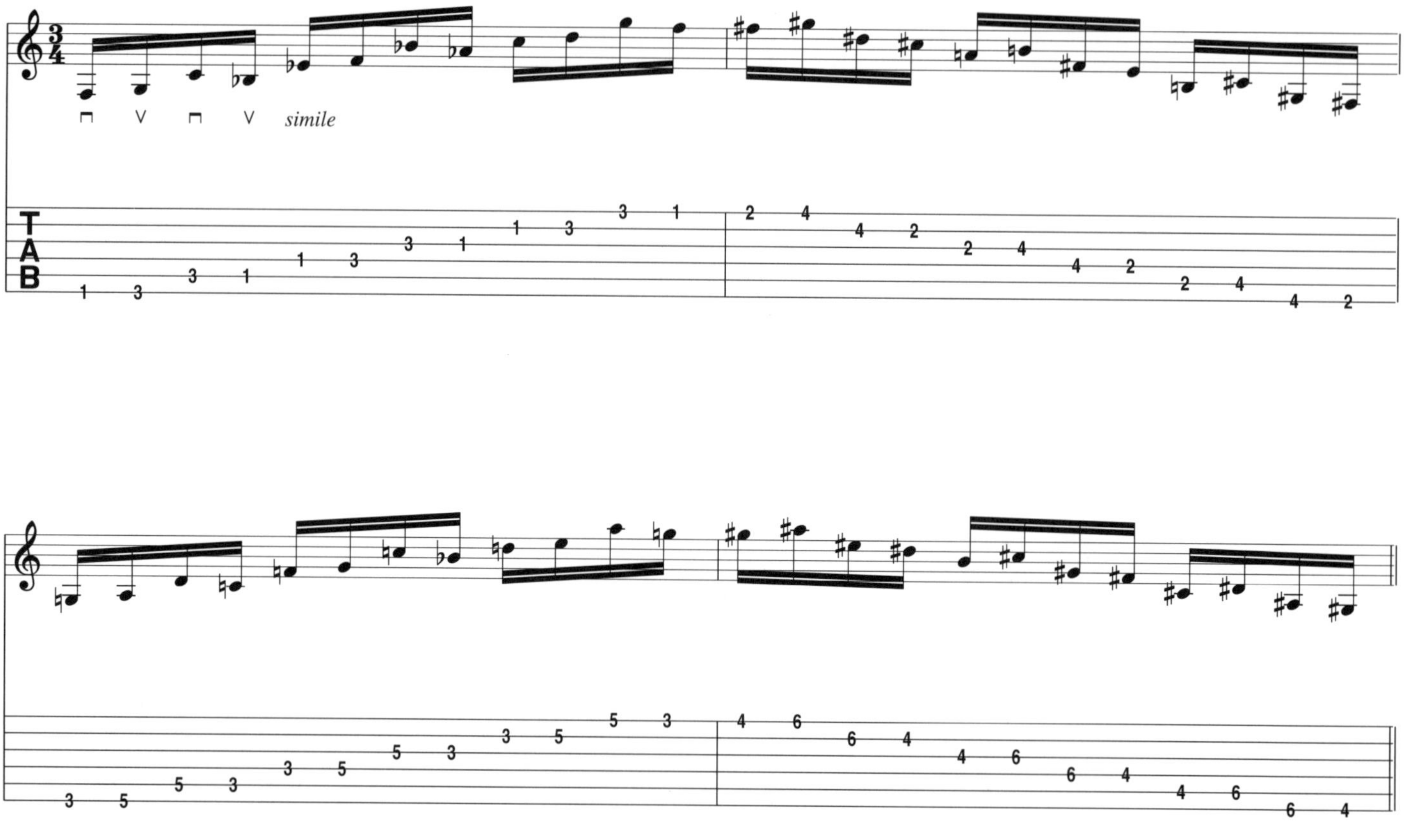

This example utilizes a three note per string pattern. Once again, take note of the optional left hand fingering.

Example 20

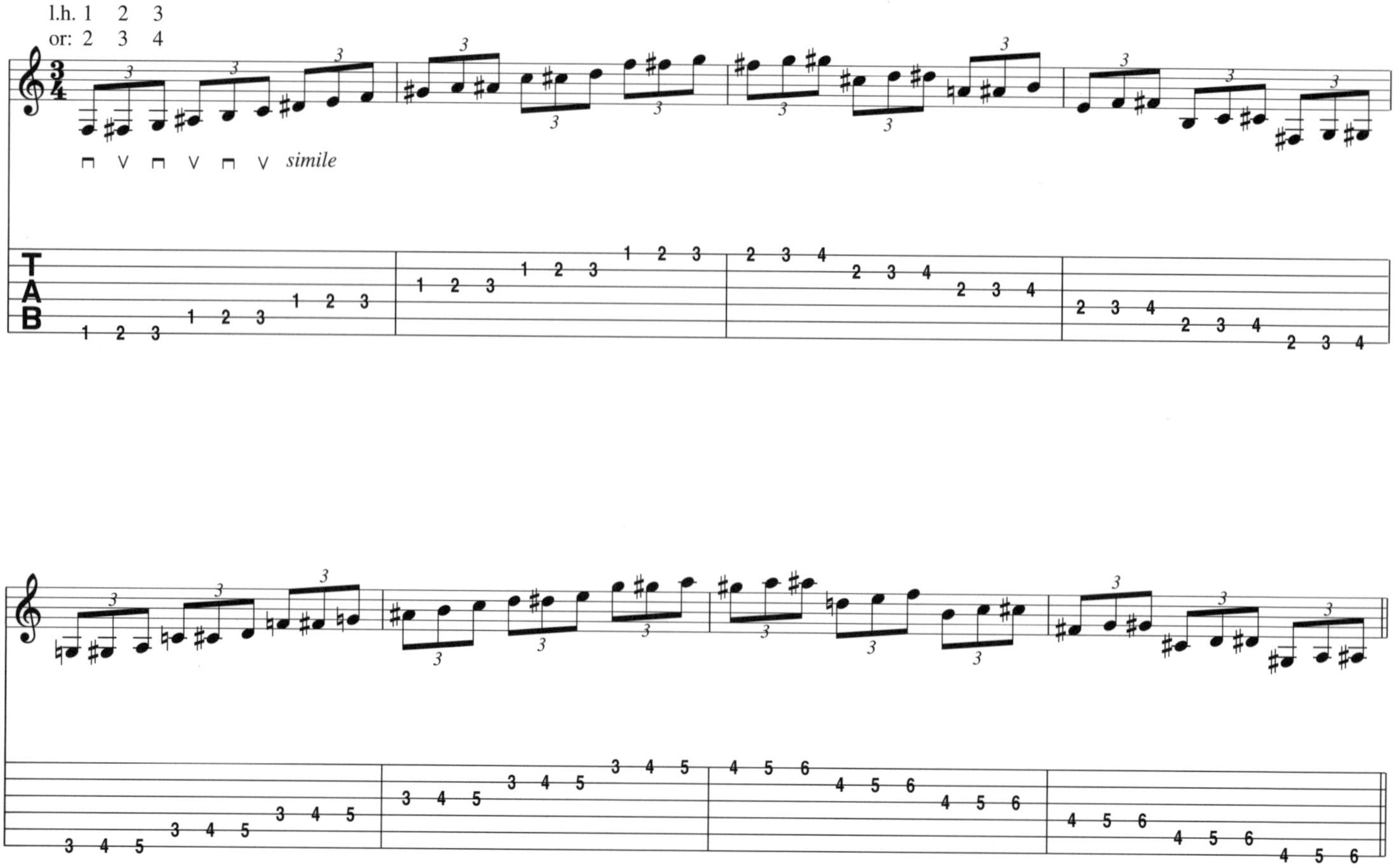

Here, let's reverse the three note sequence.

Example 21

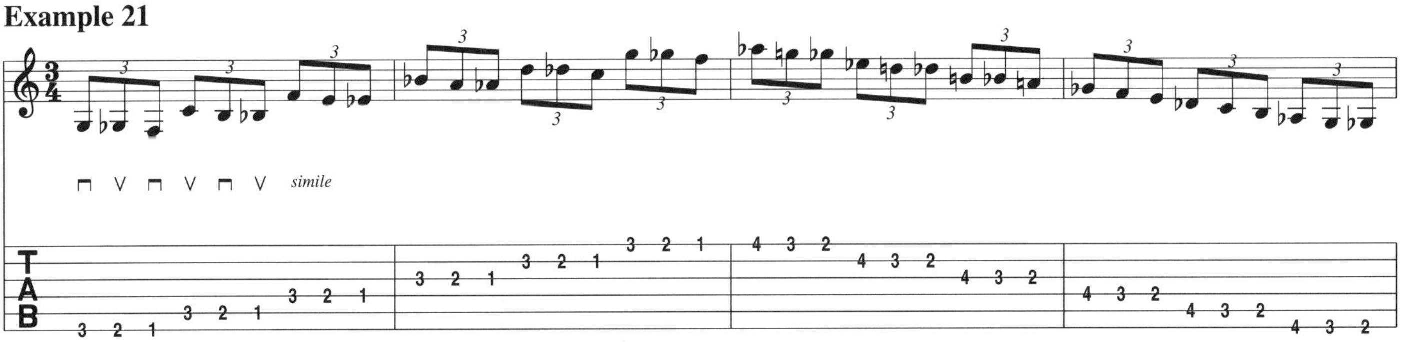

The three note per string sequences ascend and descend alternately in the next example.

Example 22

Here is a four-note-per-string pattern.

Example 23

By simply reversing the four-note sequences found in the previous example, a new exercise is created.

Example 24

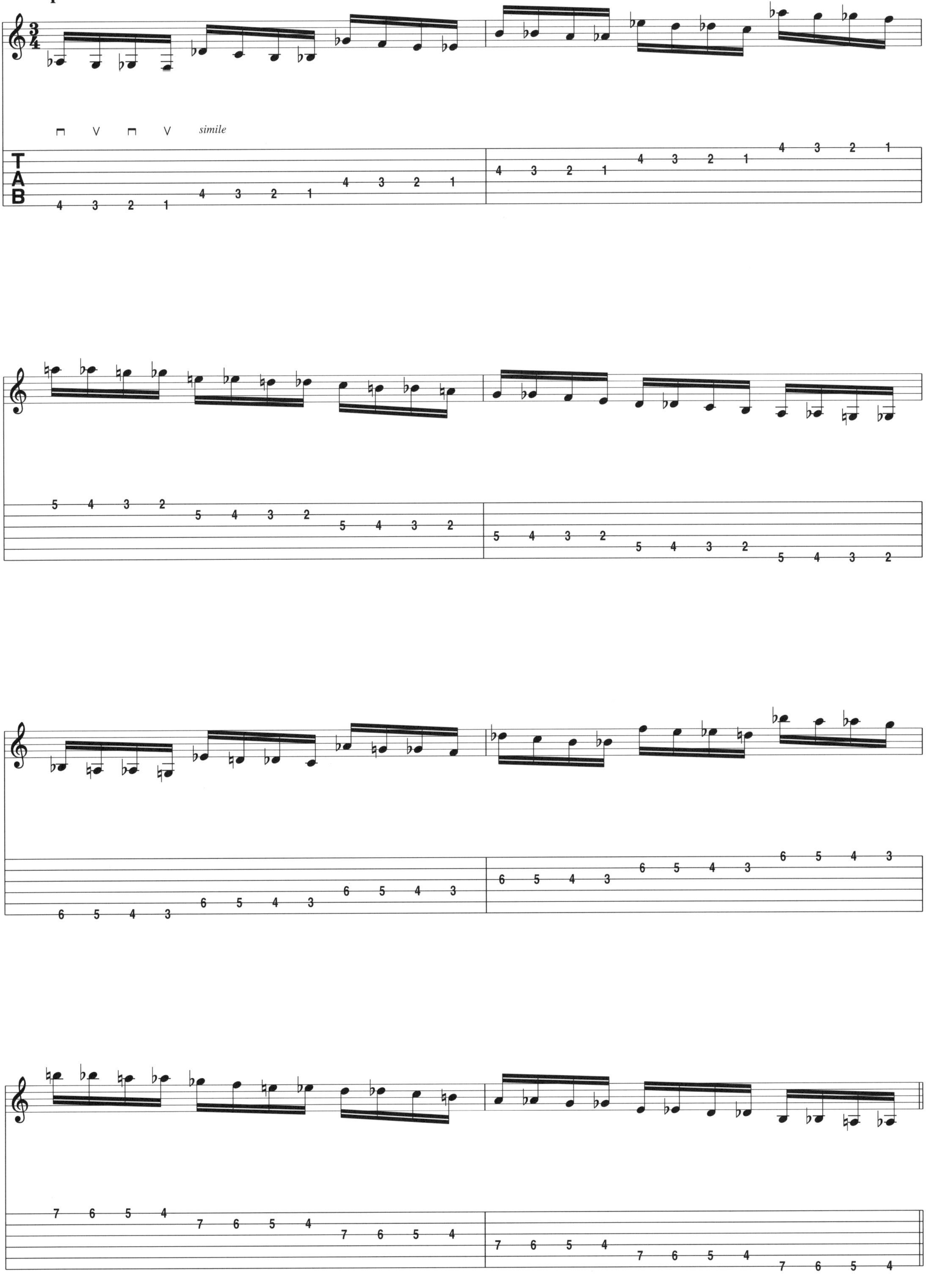

This example combines ascending and descending sequences.

Example 25

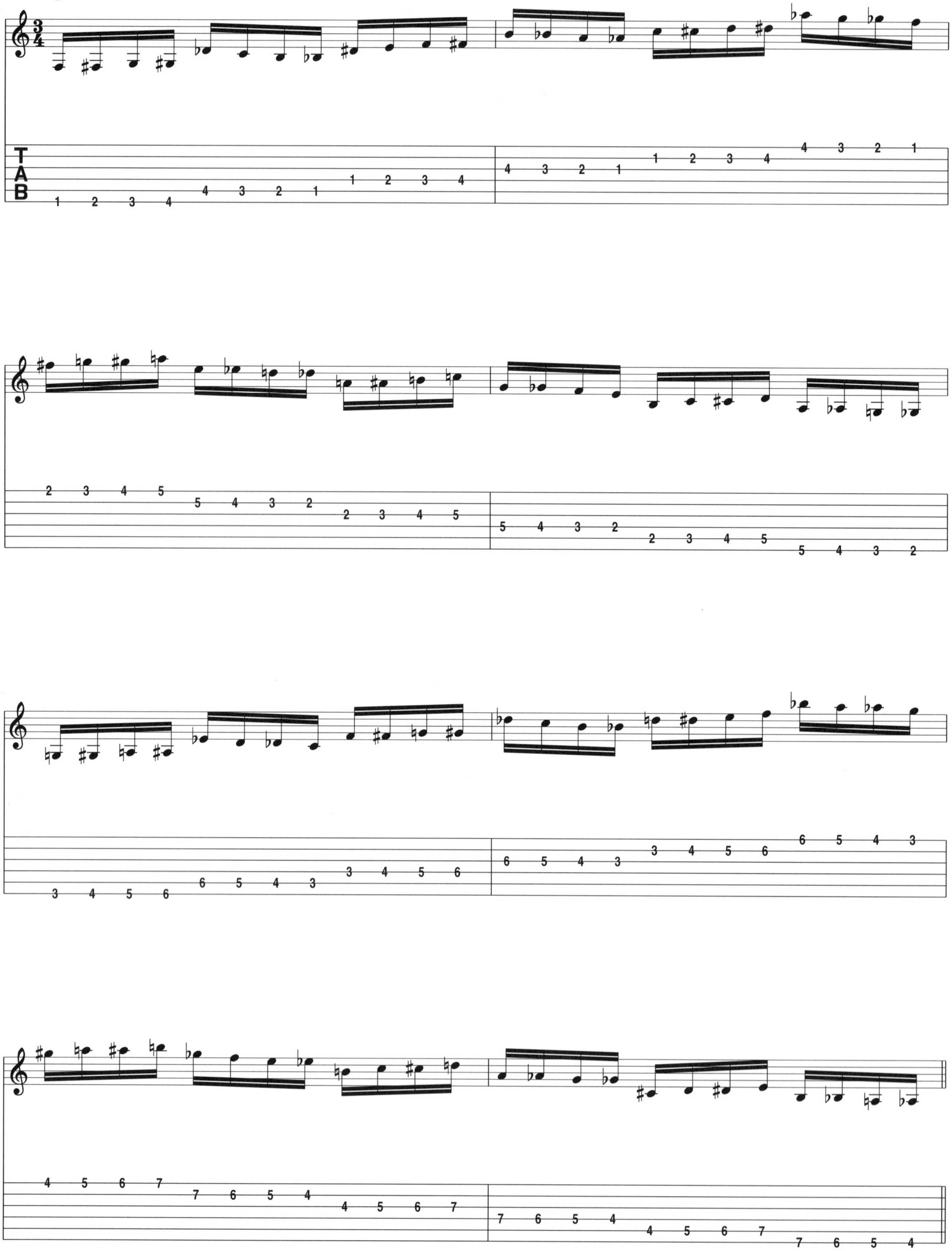

In addition to helping establish comfort and synchronization with alternate picking, Examples 17-25 make great warm-up exercises which may be included in your daily routine.

Linear Scalar Sequences

Breaking scales down into smaller, fragmented ideas (sequences) is a great way to develop your speed and synchronization, and discover some cool licks, as well. The compactness of simple sequences allows you to keep track of the accuracy of their execution. Once the basic sequences are mastered, they can become the building blocks of longer, more impressive lines.

One-String Sequences

The following examples combine for an effective method with which to develop the four-note sequence. By placing a quarter note between each repetition, the sequence is easily kept in time as you work to increase the tempo. Once a level of comfort is established, try working with two reps before pausing. Finally, try to consistently repeat the sequence, paying close attention to keeping strict time.

5 Examples 26-63

Example 26A **Example 26B** **Example 26C**

Apply the procedure from the previous examples when working on the following four-note sequences.

Example 27

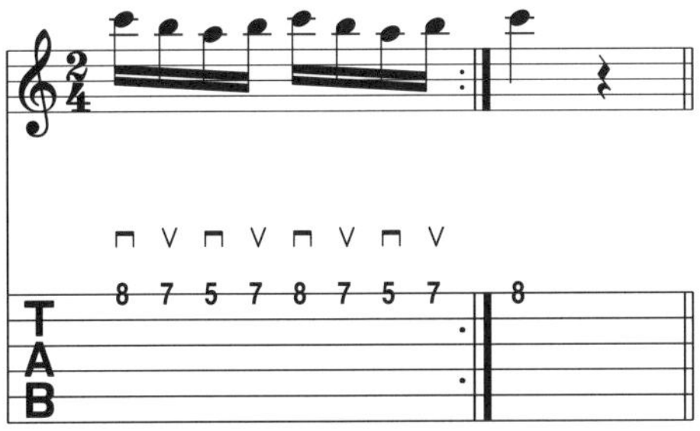

Example 28

Example 29

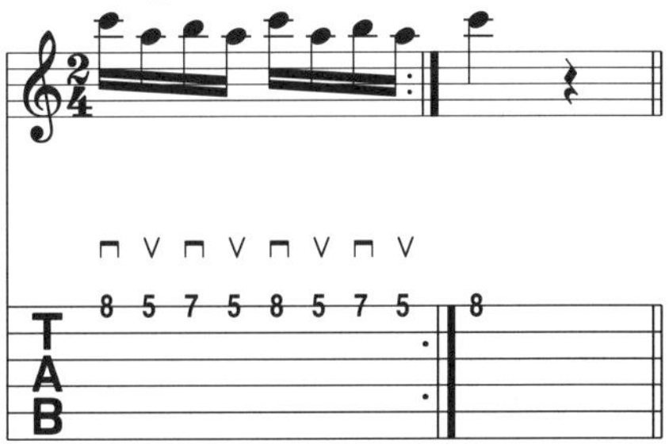

The above practice procedure may also be applied to a three-note sequence.

Example 30A **Example 30B** **Example 30C**

Here are some more three- and six-note sequences.

Example 31

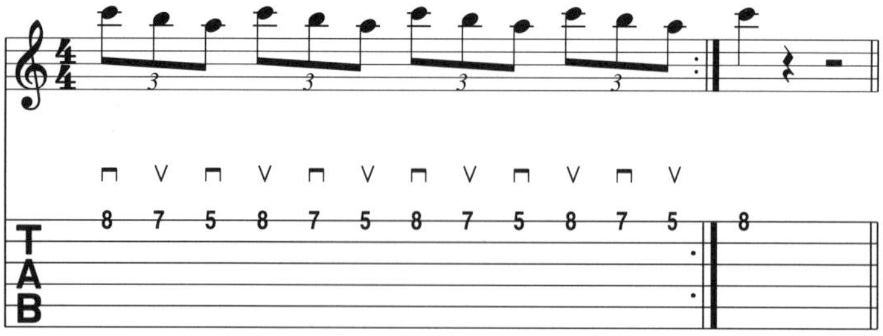

Example 32

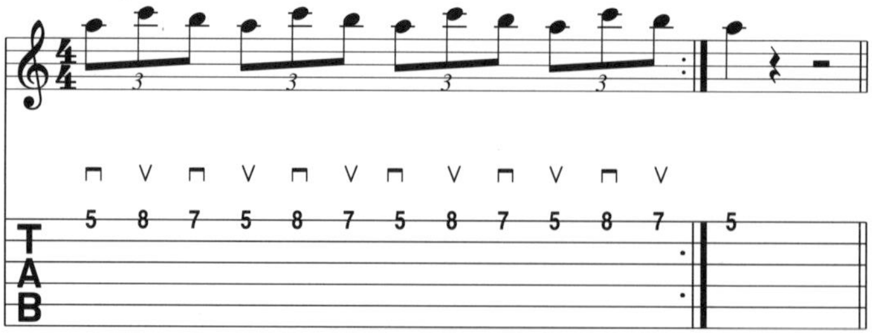

Example 33

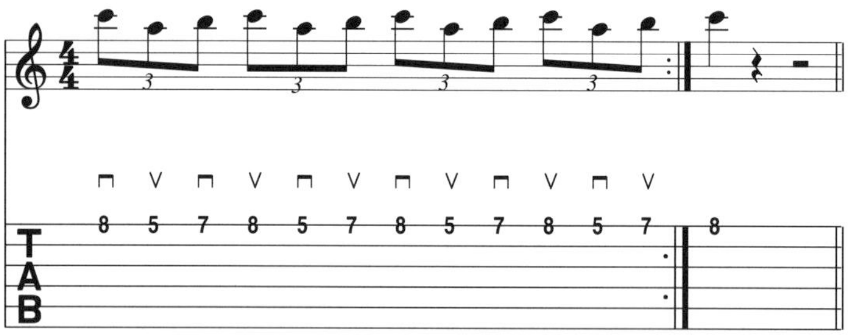

Example 34

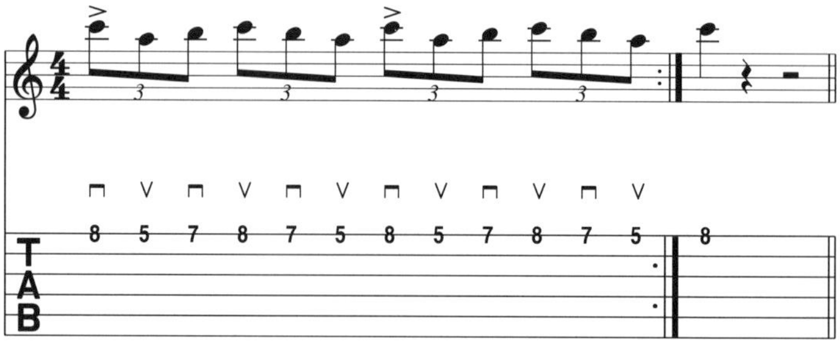

Example 35

This next example shows a four-note sequence applied in an ascending line, using the C major scale.

Example 36

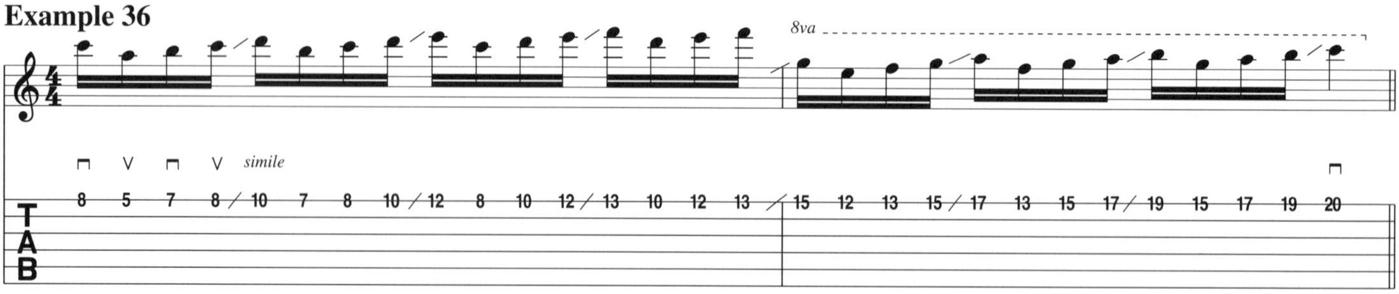

Here, we reverse direction and play the four-note sequence in a descending line.

Example 37

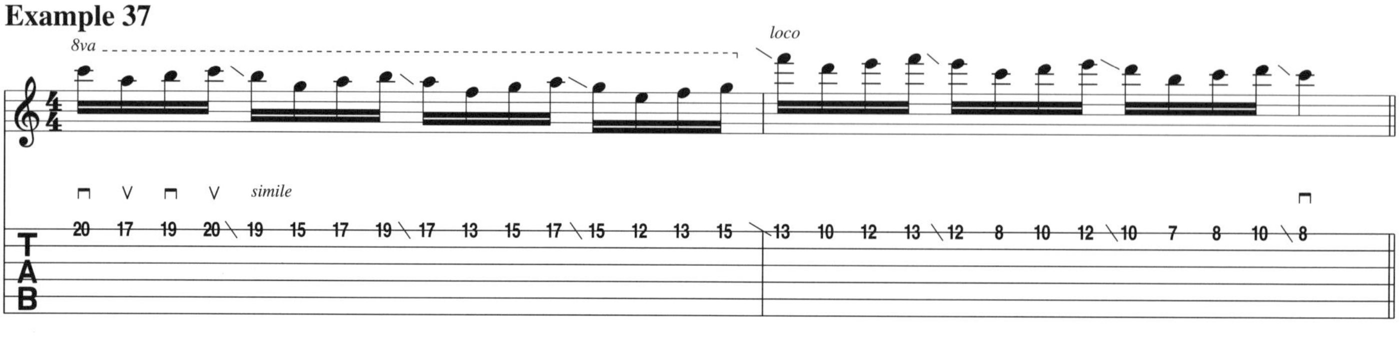

In the next example, a three-note sequence is applied in an ascending line, using the C major scale.

Example 38

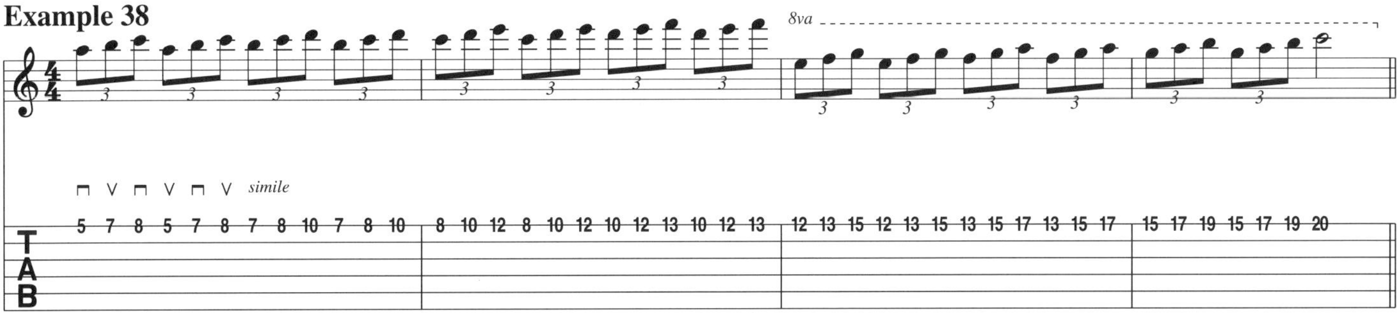

Now try playing the three-note sequence in a descending line.

Example 39

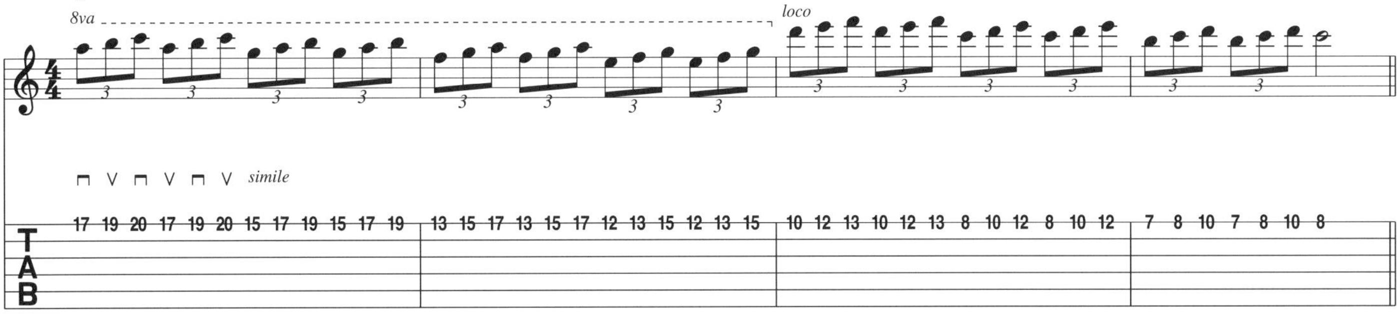

Here, we expand to playing a six-note sequence in an ascending line, using the C major scale.

Example 40

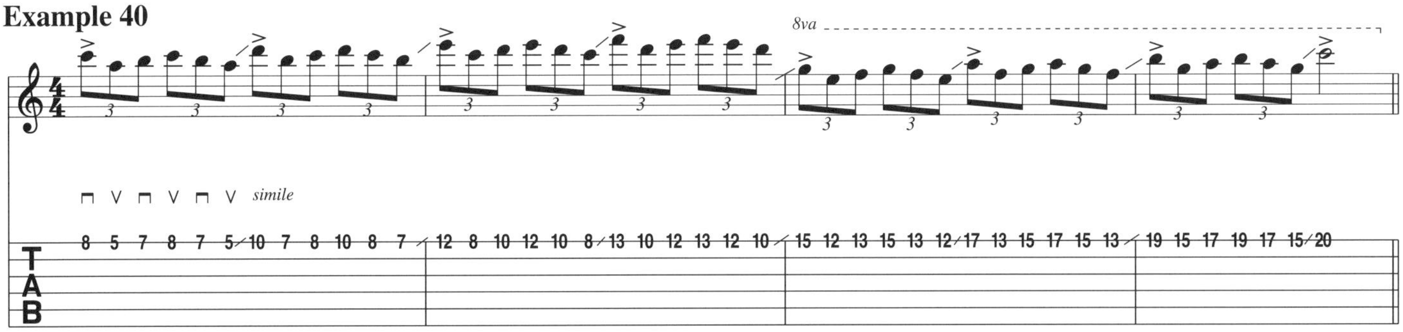

Now play the six-note sequence in a descending line.

Example 41

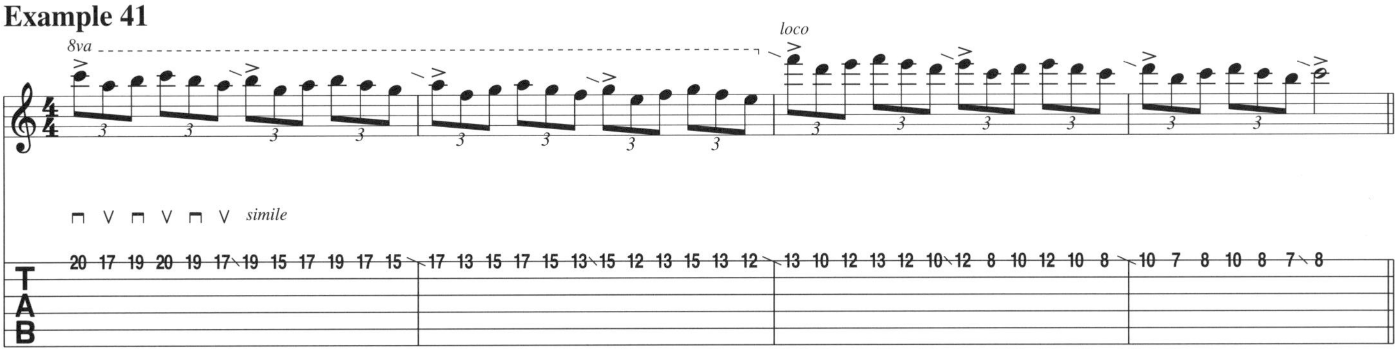

It is very important to practice each of the preceding one-string sequences on each string, since right hand positions will vary.

Two-String Sequences

The following examples apply the progressive approach for playing a two-string sequence using eighth-note triplets. When making the transition between strings, take special care to keep the correct alternate picking. Once this transition becomes second nature, gradually work to increase the tempo.

Example 42A

Example 42B

Example 42C

Apply the preceding approach to the following triplet sequences.

Example 43

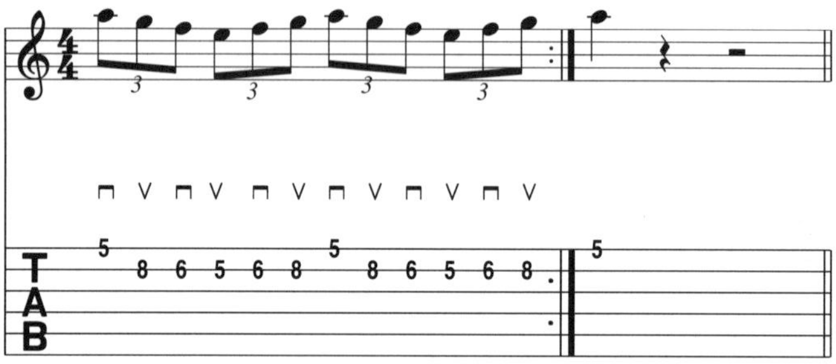

Example 44

Example 45

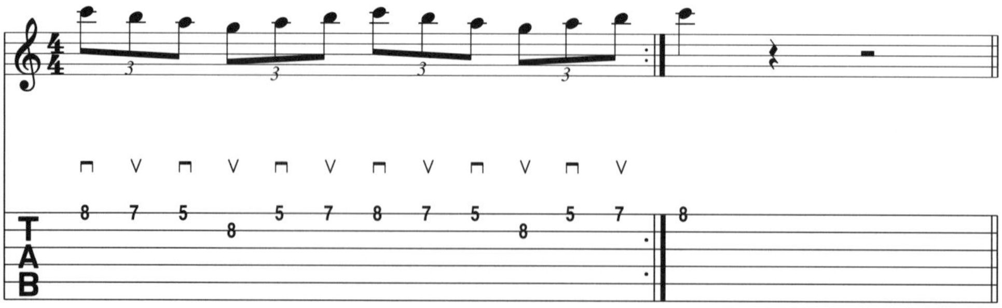

Example 46

Example 47

Example 48

Example 49

The following examples apply the progressive approach for playing a two-string sequence using sixteenth notes.

Example 50A

Example 50B

Example 50C

Apply the preceding approach to the following sixteenth note sequences.

Example 51

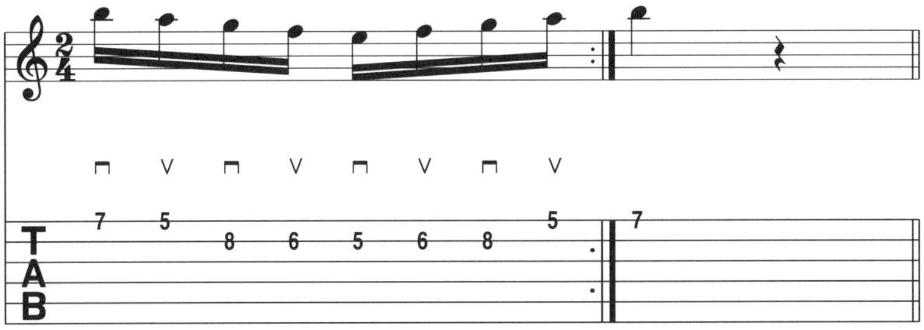

Example 52

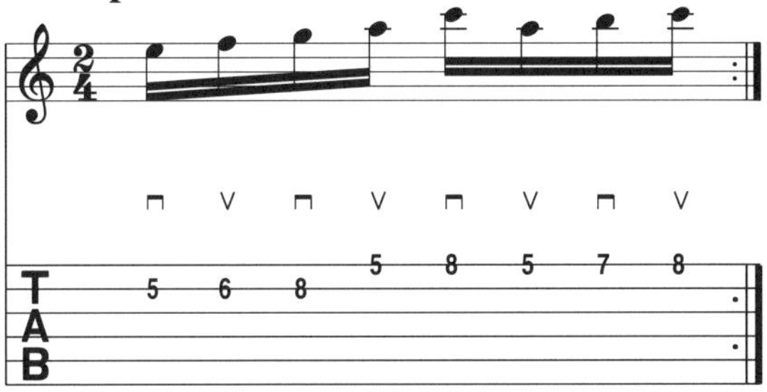

Example 53

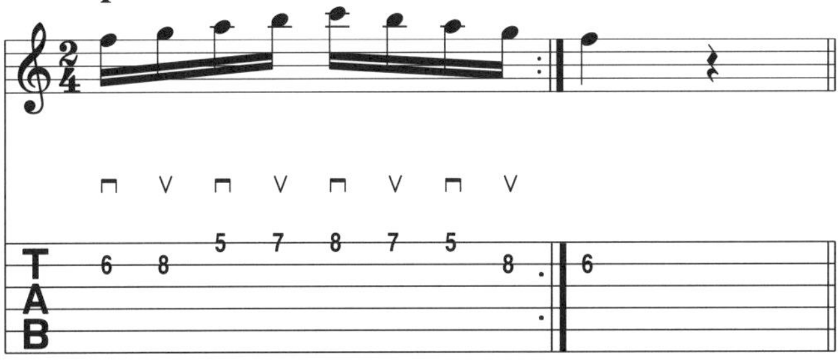

Example 54

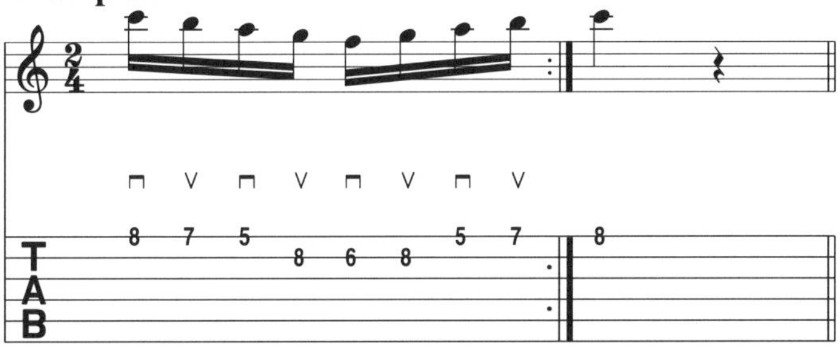

Example 55

Example 56

The longer sequences shown in the following examples utilize material from previous examples. Notice how we have used short simple sequences to build longer lines.

Example 57

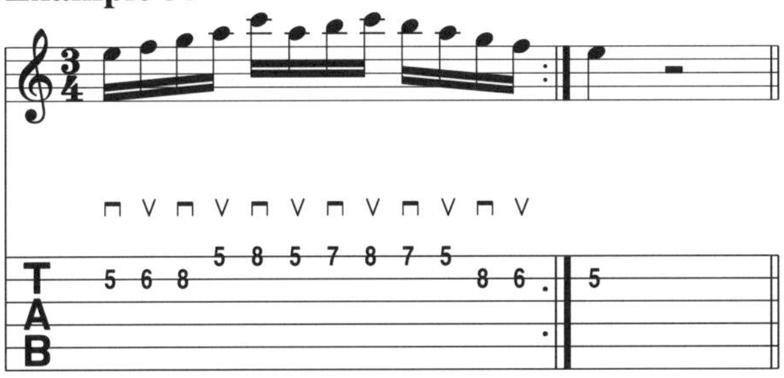

Example 58

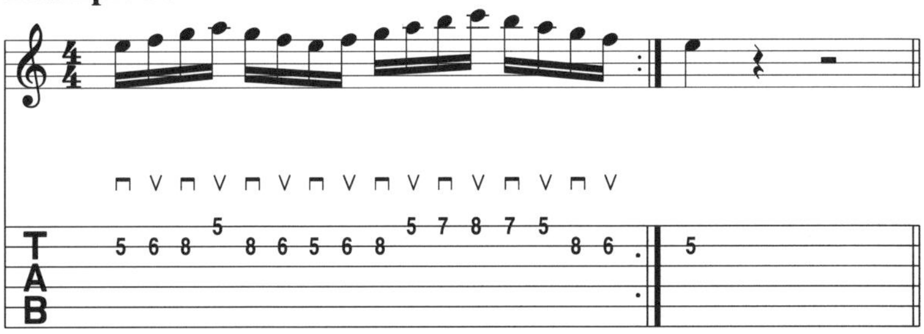

The following examples utilize variations of the triplet sequences found in Examples 48 and 49. Be patient and precise when working on these longer sequences.

Example 59

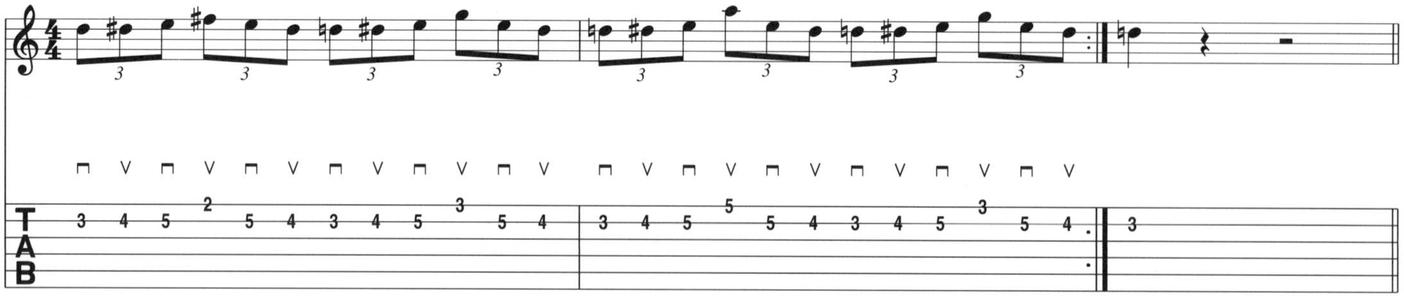

Example 60

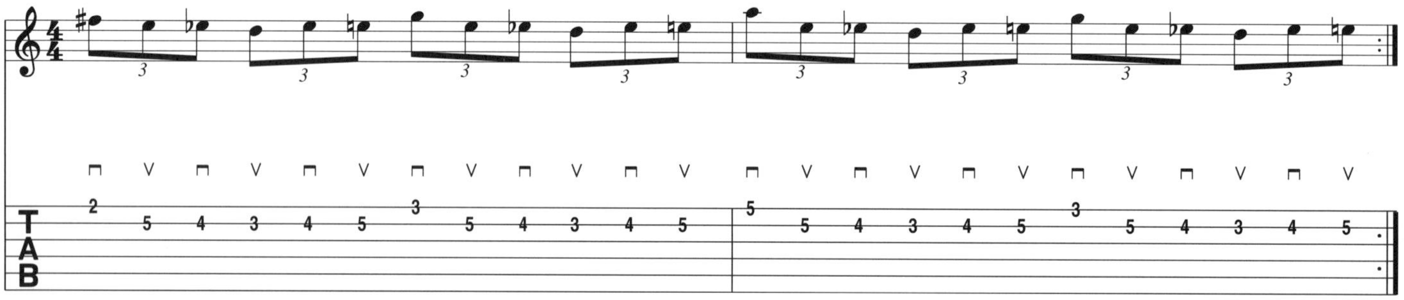

Example 61

Example 62

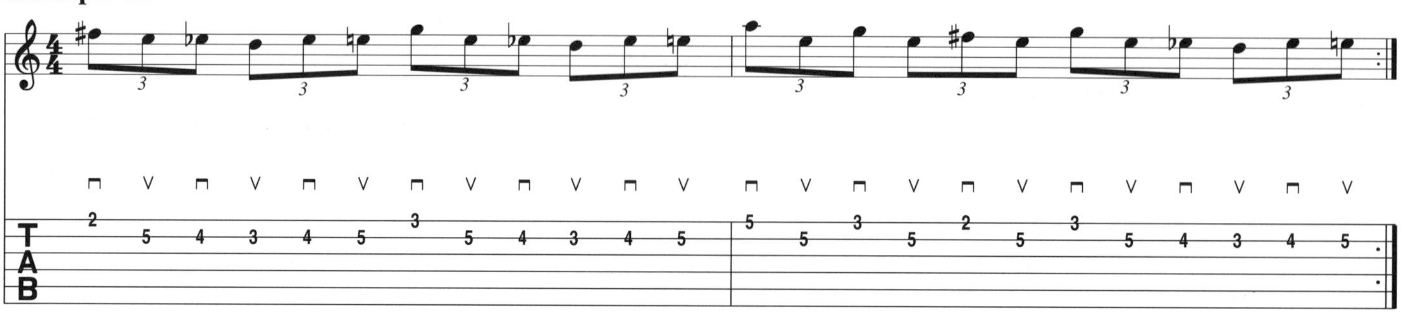

Try applying each of the two-string sequences to each pair of strings for further practice.

This example illustrates the application of a two-string sequence to ascending and descending lines in C major.

Example 63

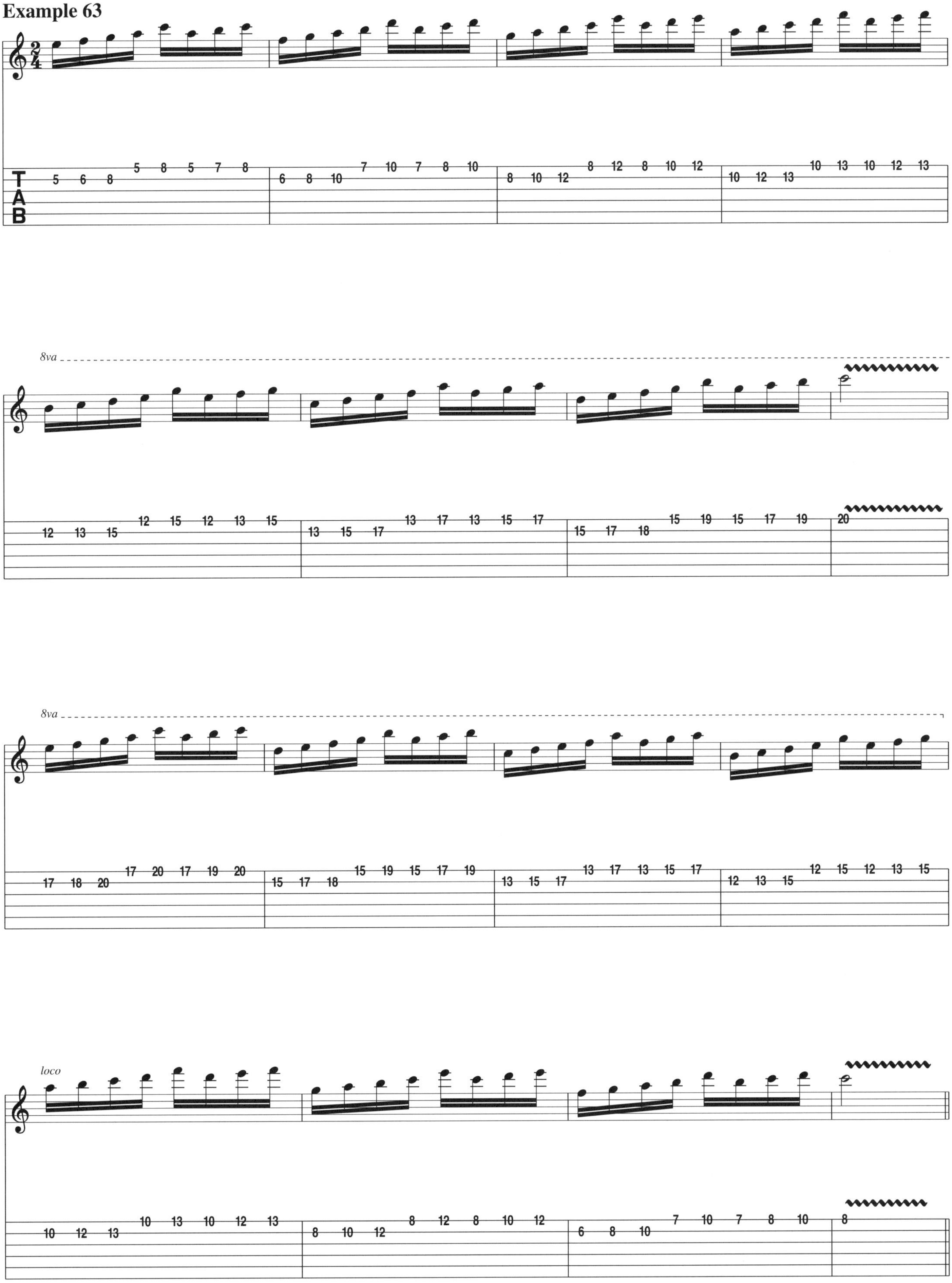

Try playing this exercise using all twelve major scales on each pair of strings.

Positional Scalar Sequences

The positional scale sequences shown here utilize a three-note per string G major scale. Once the basic sequences are mastered, they should be applied to all seven patterns in all twelve keys (see scale appendix for patterns).

The next examples illustrate ascending and descending scalar passages. Lines that move rapidly across all six strings are difficult to gain control of. Practice patiently and slowly. Accenting the downbeats will help you maintain rhythm and clarity.

6 Examples 64-84

Example 64

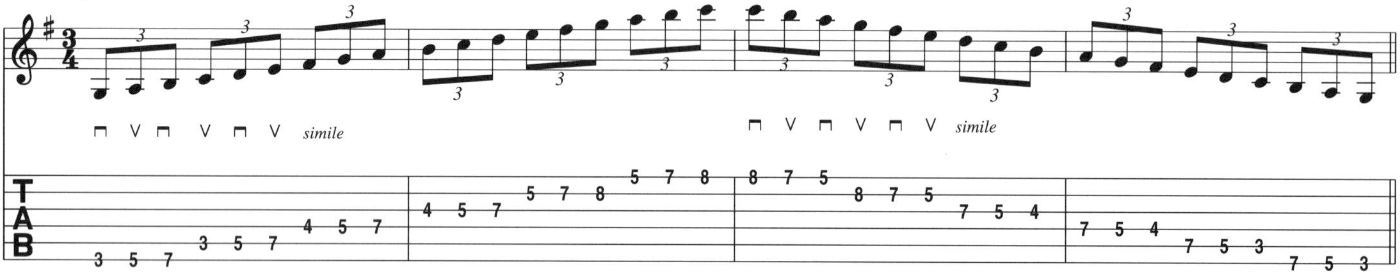

Example 65

The following examples illustrate lines that incorporate one- and two-string sequences into positional playing.

Example 66A

Example 66B

Example 67A

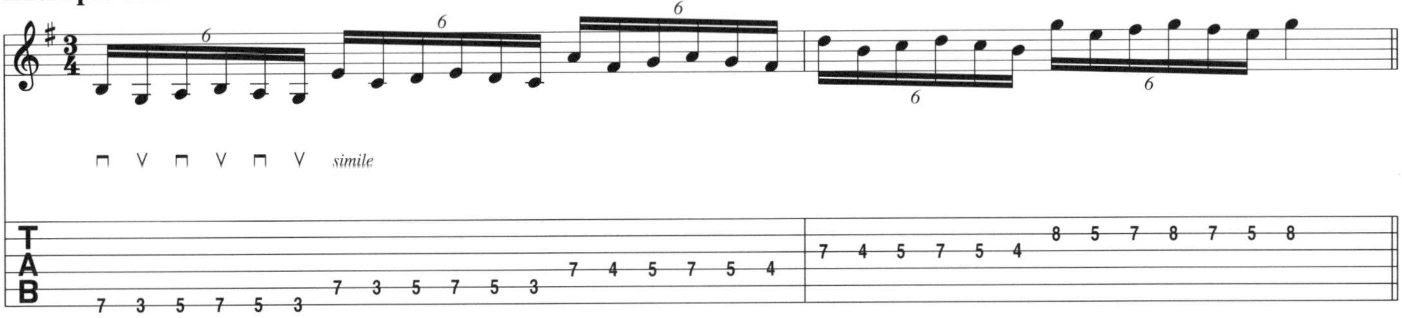

Example 67B

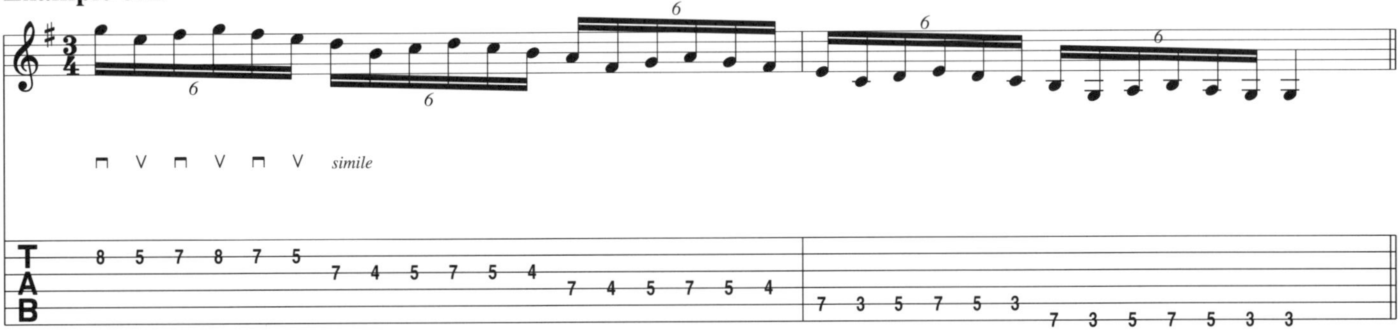

The concept of intervallic skipping offers many challenging possibilities. The following exercises utilize a variety of intervallic sequences. Take care to maintain strict alternate picking throughout.

Example 68A G major scale in 3rds, ascending

Example 68B G major scale in 3rds, descending

Example 69A G major scale in inverted 2nds, ascending

Example 69B G major scale in inverted 2nds, descending

In the next set of examples, a simple polyrhythm is implied as the G major scale in 3rds, usually felt as pairs of notes, is played as triplets.

Example 70A G major scale in 3rds, ascending triplets

Example 70B G major scale in 3rds, descending triplets

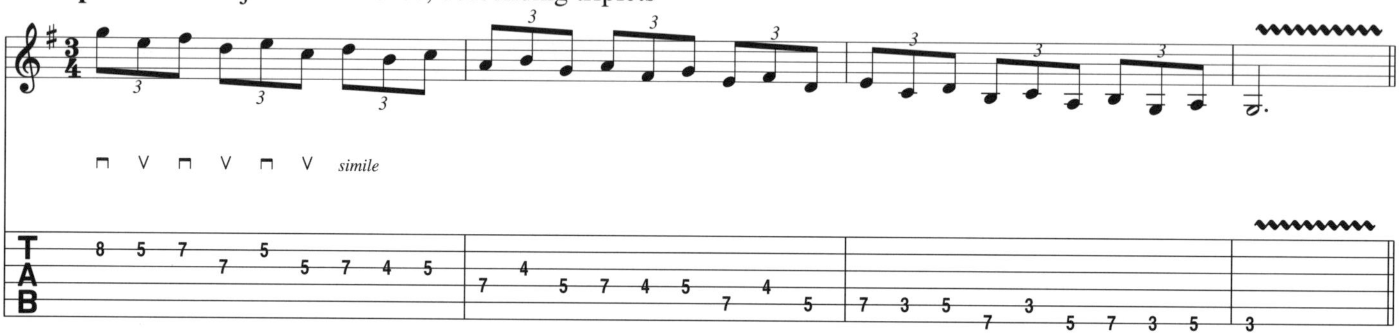

Example 71A G major scale in inverted 2nds, ascending

Example 71B G major scale in inverted 2nds, descending

In the following examples, the 3rds are alternately inverted, for yet another variation.

Example 72A G major scale in 3rds, alternately inverted, ascending

Example 72B G major scale in 3rds, alternately inverted, descending

The following examples illustrate the basic sequences for playing intervals for 4ths, 5ths, & 6ths, respectively. Try the variations shown for 3rds on these sequences, as well.

Example 73A G major scale in 4ths, ascending

Example 73B G major scale in 4ths, descending

Example 74A G major scale in 5ths, ascending

Example 74B G major scale in 5ths, descending

Example 75A G major scale in 6ths, ascending

Example 75B G major scale in 6ths, descending

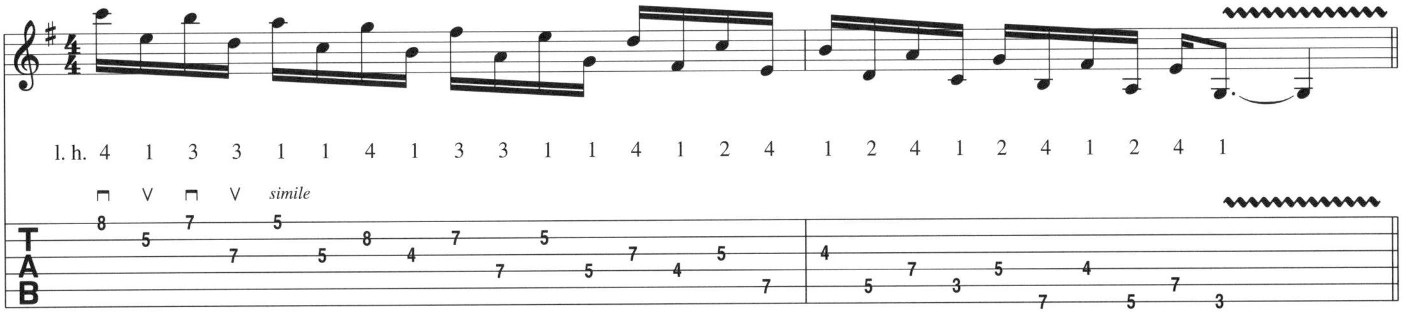

Once these basic intervallic sequences have been mastered in the scale position shown, they should be applied to each of the remaining 3-note-per-string patterns as well as all twelve major keys. Examples 76 and 77 illustrate the basic "ascending 3rds" sequence applied to two alternate G major scale positions (patterns 2 & 3) the 3-note-per-string patterns in the appendix.

Example 76

Example 77

Once you can comfortably sequence in each scale pattern, all the patterns in each key can be connected, in order to cover the fretboard in any key. Playing through all the patterns successively will not only increase your knowledge of the fretboard, but give you a great alternate picking workout, as well. Take each of the following examples up and back through all seven scale patterns in all twelve keys.

Example 78 C major

Example 79 C major

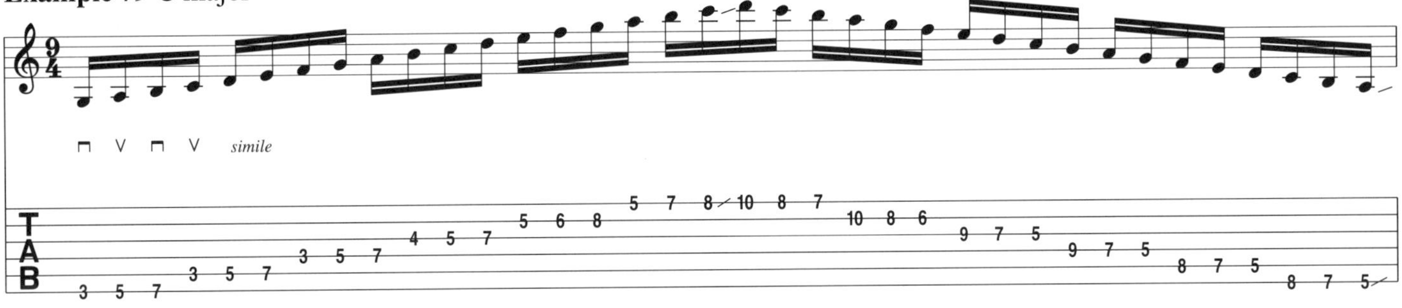

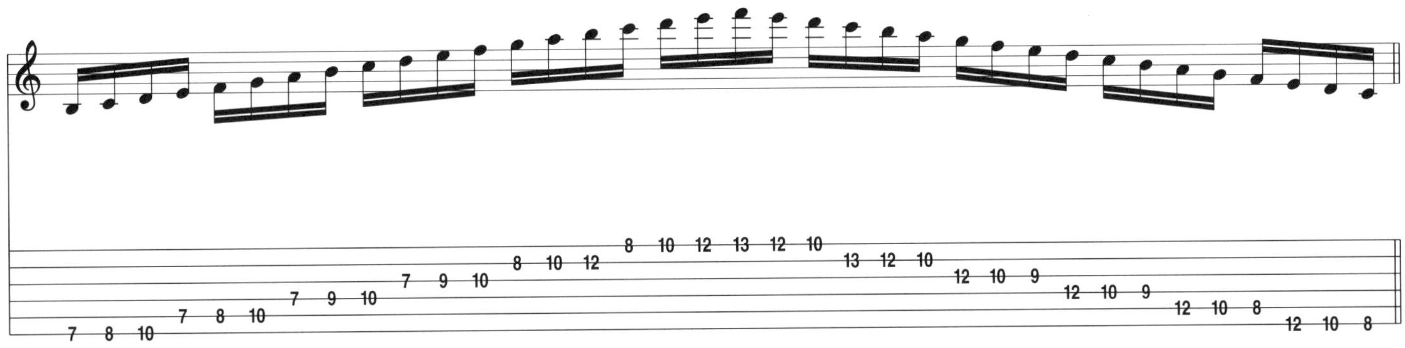

The intervallic sequencing concepts we've worked on can be utilized in these fretboard workouts, as well. Remember to connect all the positions in each key.

Example 80 C major, in 3rds

Mathematical grouping is another type of sequencing that can be very effective in the development of alternate picking. In this type of sequencing, a scale fragment of designated length (the examples here use 3 and 4 note groups) starts on each note of the scale.

Example 81 C major, groups of 3, triplets

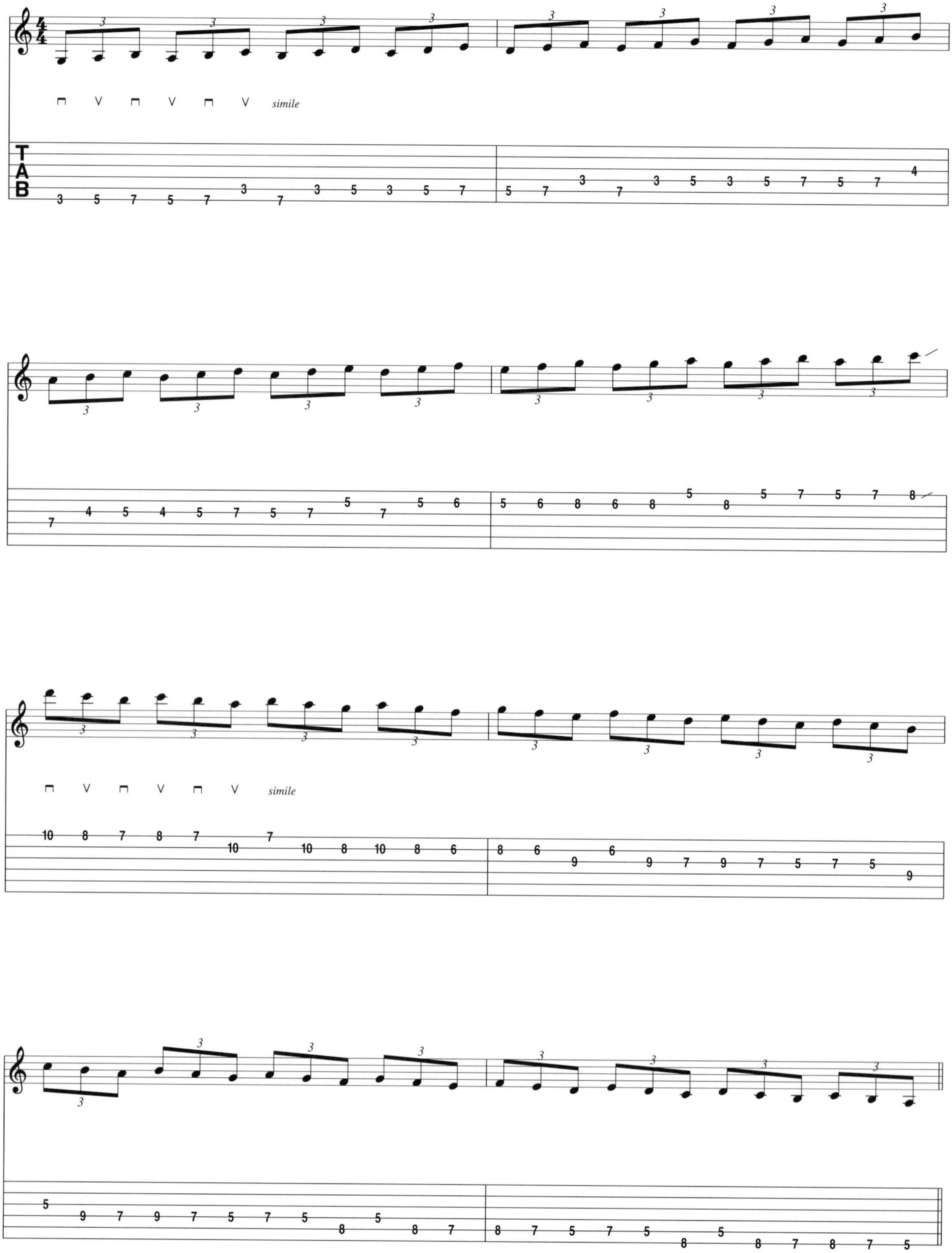

The effect of a simple polyrhythm is created when the groups of three are played against a sixteenth-note rhythm.

Example 82 C major, groups of 3, sixteenths

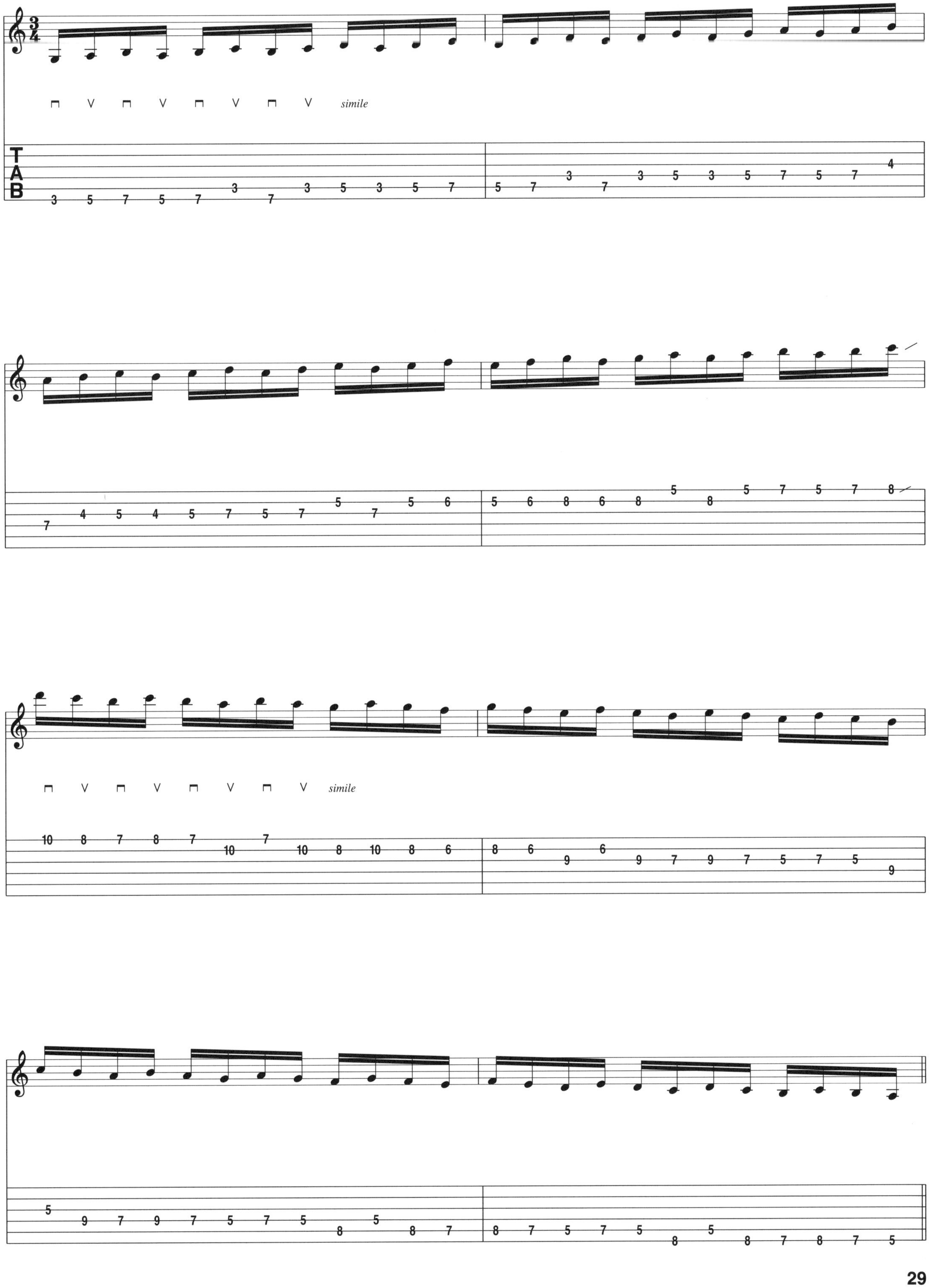

A basic mathematical sequence in groups of four may also be played in any key.

Example 83 C major, groups of 4, sixteenths

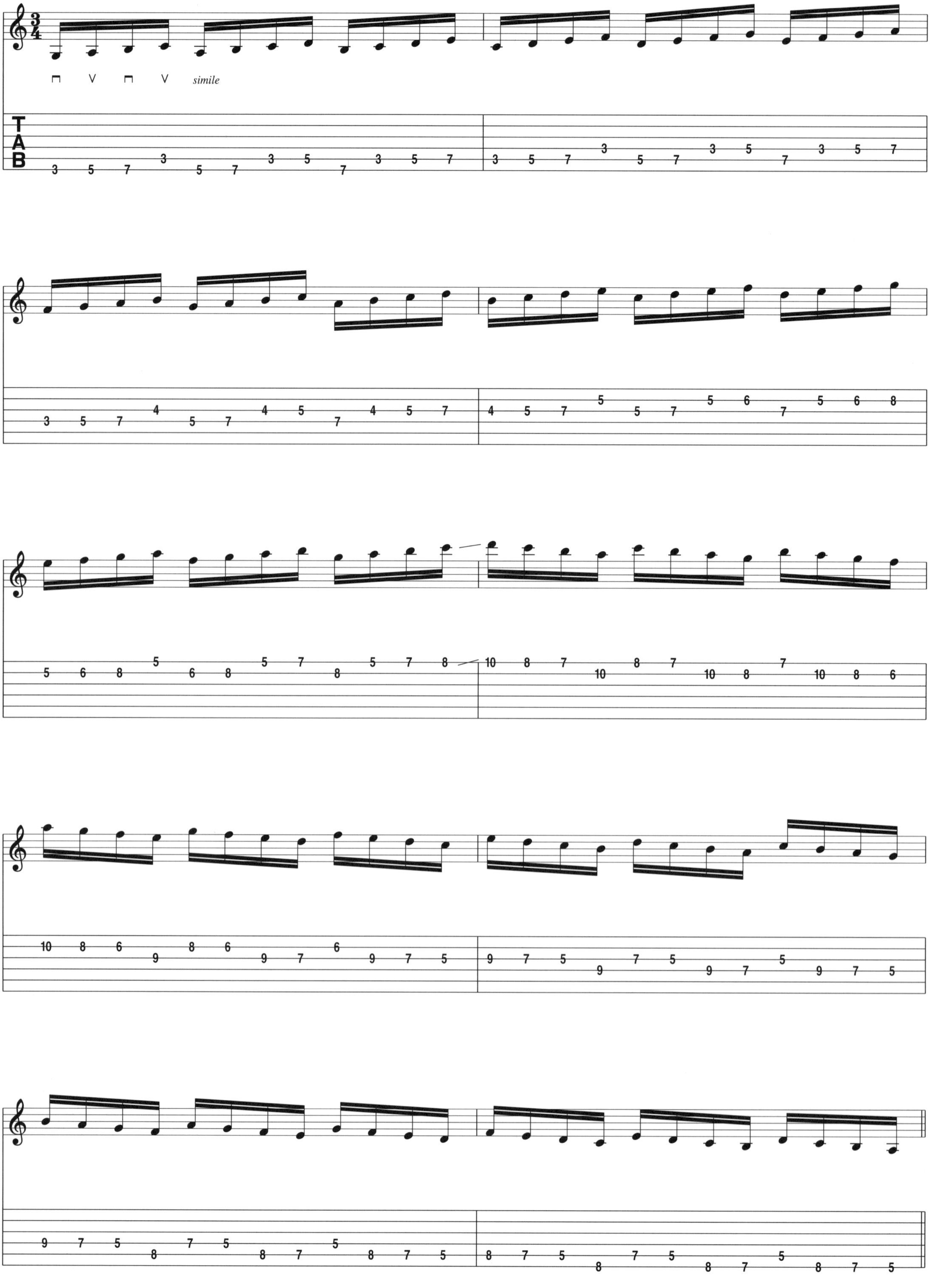

The effect of another simple polyrhythm is created when the groups of four are played against a triplet rhythm.

Example 84 C major, groups of 4, triplets

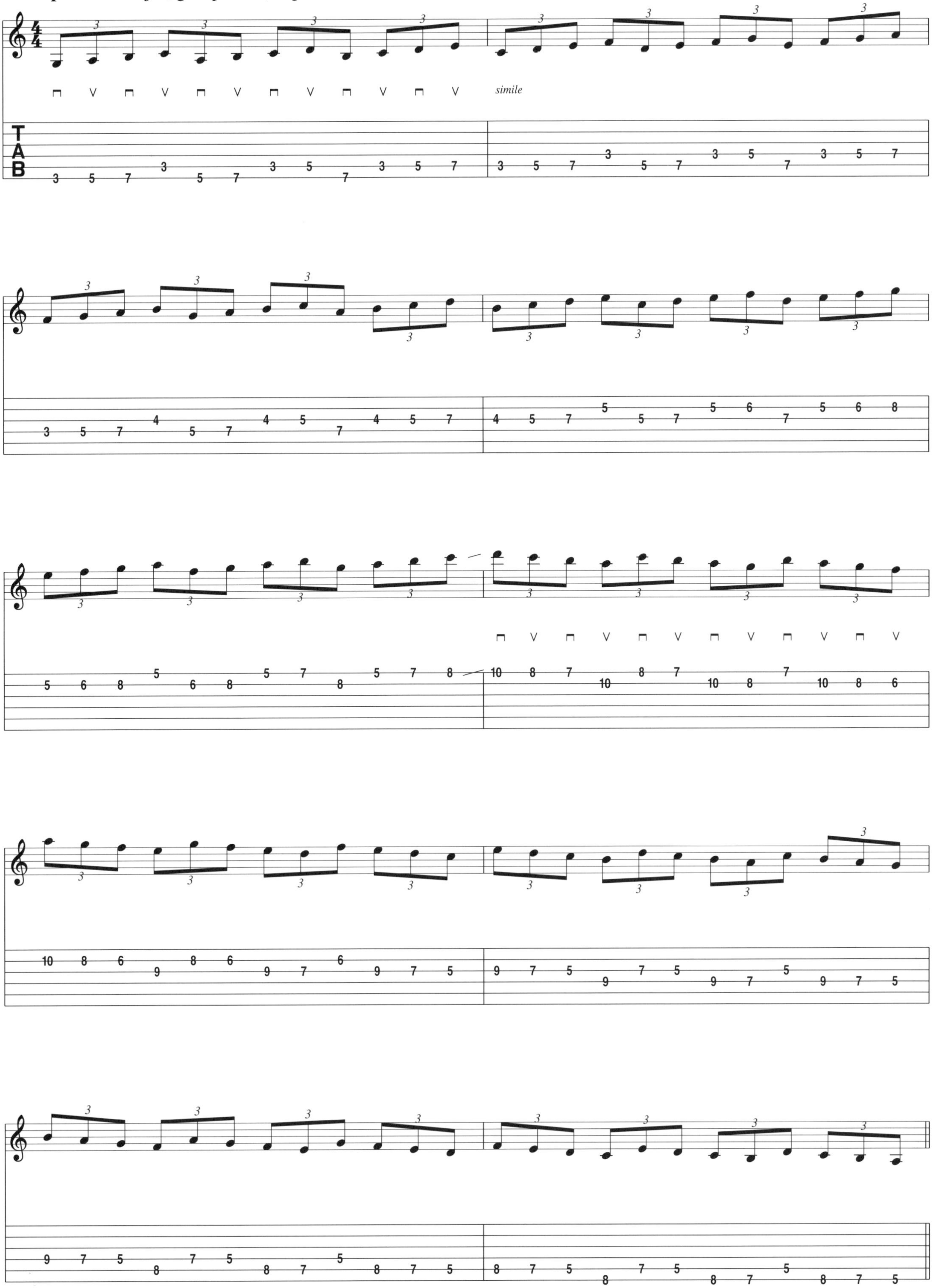

Pentatonic Scalar Sequences

Now, let's apply alternate picking to the pentatonic scale. The following examples utilize the common minor pentatonic "box" pattern and move up chromatically in the same manner as the symmetrical patterns shown earlier. Connect each position as shown, ascending the neck to the twelfth position before traveling back down. Watch those pick strokes!

7 Examples 85-92

Example 85 Minor pentatonic scale in triplets

Example 86 Minor pentatonic scale in sixteenths

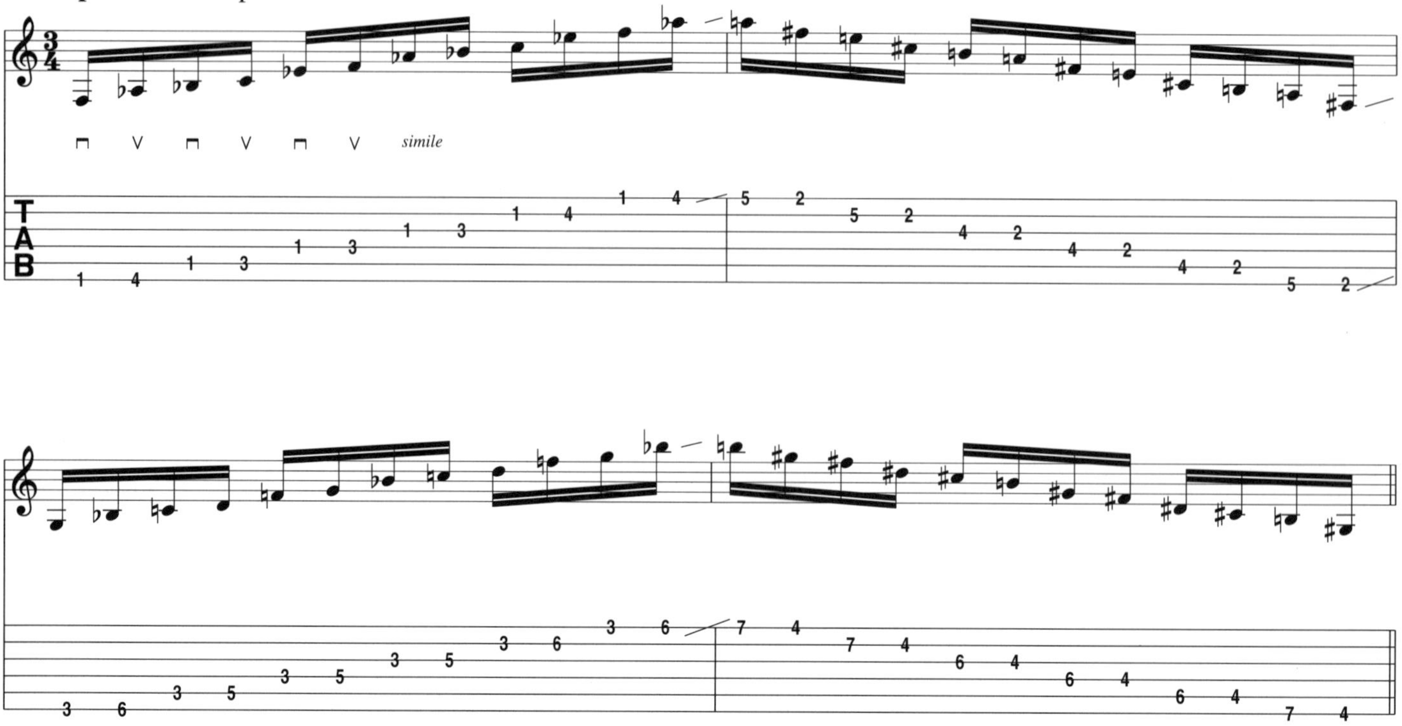

Example 87 Minor pentatonic scale in triplets, using groups of three

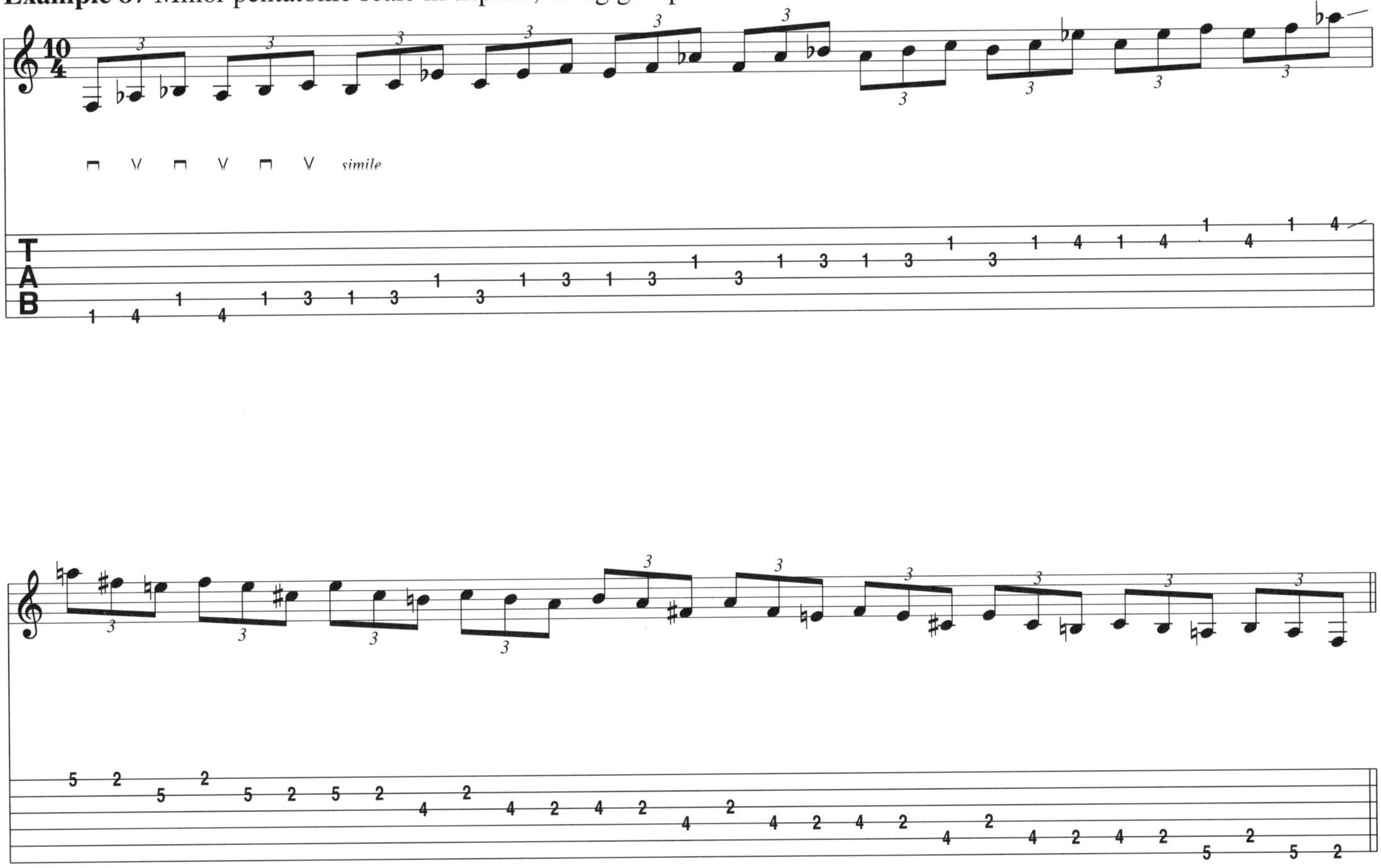

Example 88 Minor pentatonic scale in triplets, using inverted groups of three

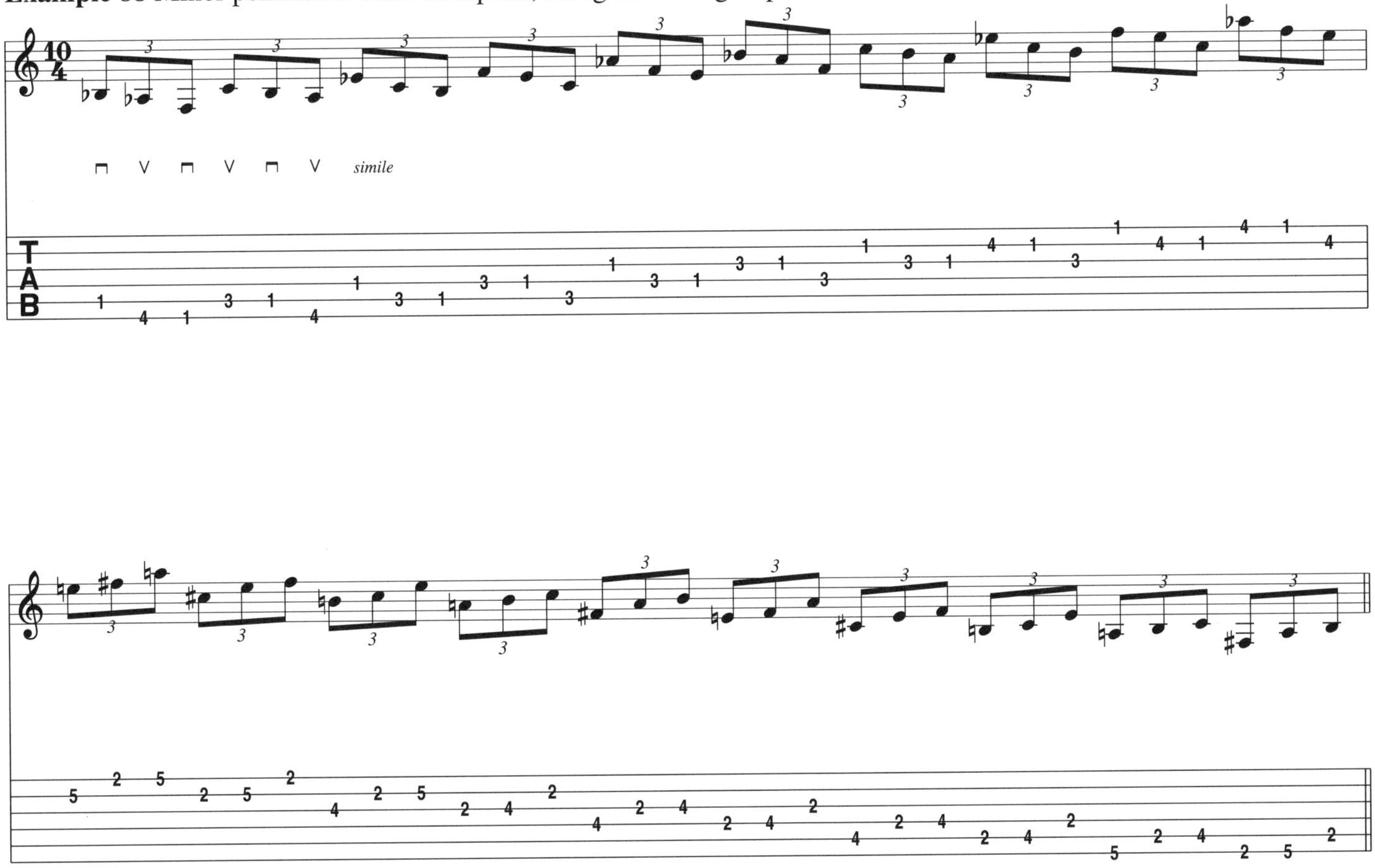

Example 89 Minor pentatonic scale in sixteenths, using groups of four

Example 90 Minor pentatonic scale in sixteenths, using inverted groups of four

Here, we introduce a new rhythm. Sixteenth-note quintuplets simply consist of five sixteenth notes per beat.

Example 91 Minor pentatonic scale in sixteenth-note quintuplets, using groups of five

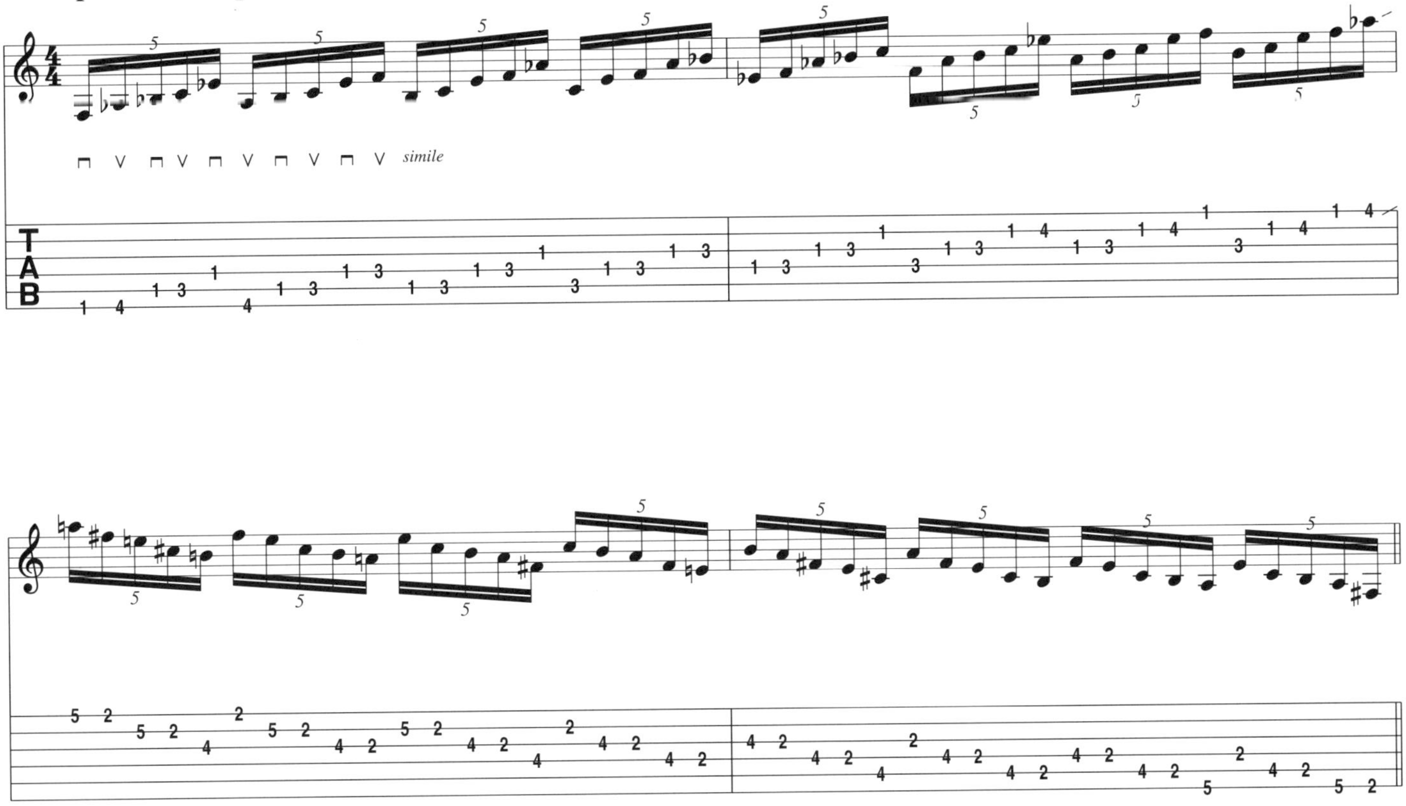

...and yet another new rhythm. Sixteenth-note sextuplets have six sixteenth notes in every beat.

Example 92 Minor pentatonic scale in sixteenth-note sextuplets, using groups of six

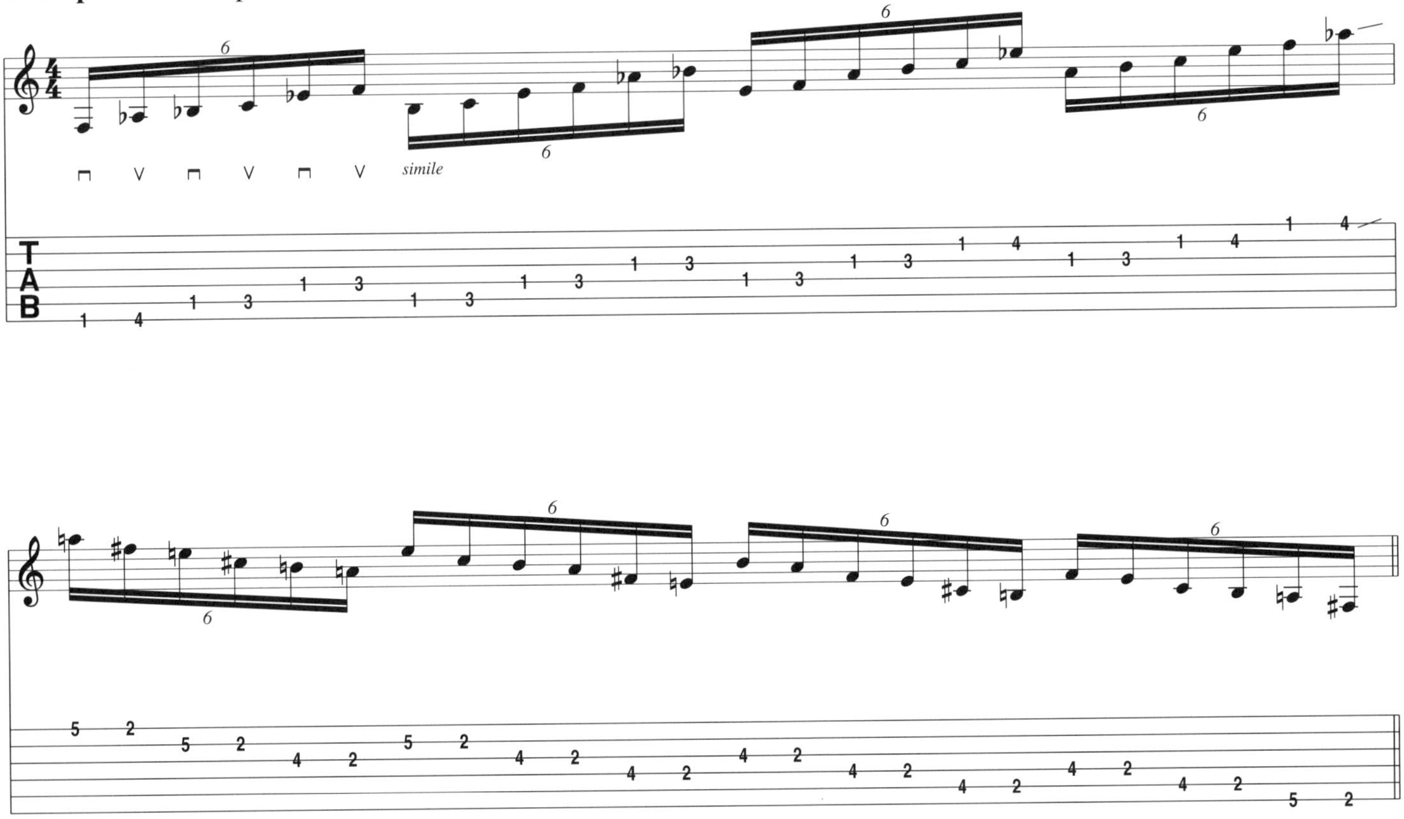

Once the preceding pentatonic sequences have been mastered, try applying them to the other 2-note-per-string pentatonic patterns (see appendix).

Alternate Picking Arpeggios

Chord Shape Arpeggiation

Until now, we have been solely concerned with applying alternate picking to linear material. However, alternate picking is indispensable for more vertical applications, as well. The most common of these vertical applications is the arpeggio.

The simplest definition of an arpeggio is the notes of a chord played separately. Let's take a look at Example 93A, in which the basic E chord is broken apart by a slow strum, using all downstrokes. This may be the most economical way to arpeggiate the chord, but the individual notes don't have a lot of definition. Now, try Example 93B. Crossing the strings with alternate picking can be a difficult technique to develop, but I think you can hear the benefits in clarity and rhythmic articulation immediately.

8 Examples 93-117

Example 93A

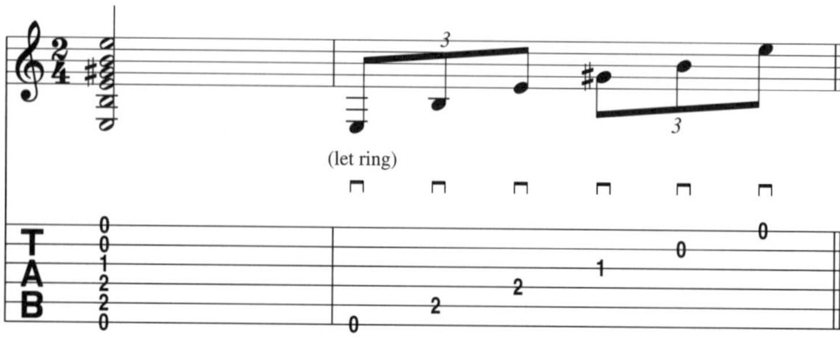

Example 93B

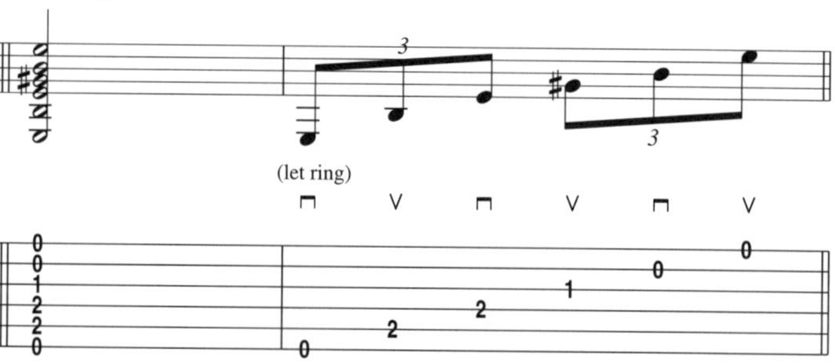

Examples 94-103 illustrate various sequences of the open position A major chord. Pay very close attention to your right hand in these exercises, since it is easy to lose the correct alternation.

Example 94

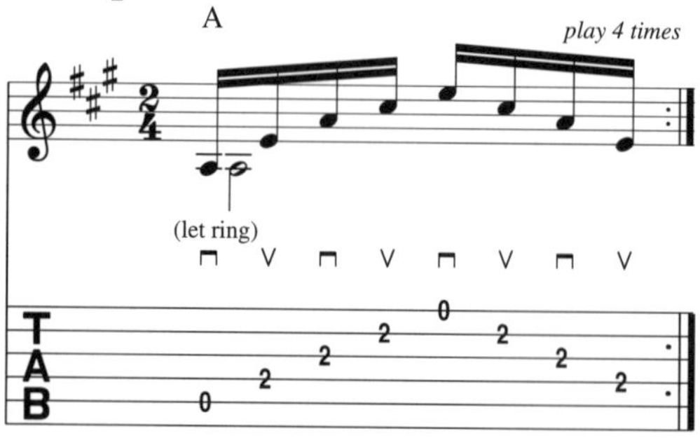

Example 95

Example 96

Example 97

Example 98

Example 99

Example 100

Example 101

Example 102

Example 103

The following is an alternate picking arpeggio study that applies a common sequence throughout. Once you've mastered it, try applying each of the sequences from Examples 94-103 to the progression.

Example 104

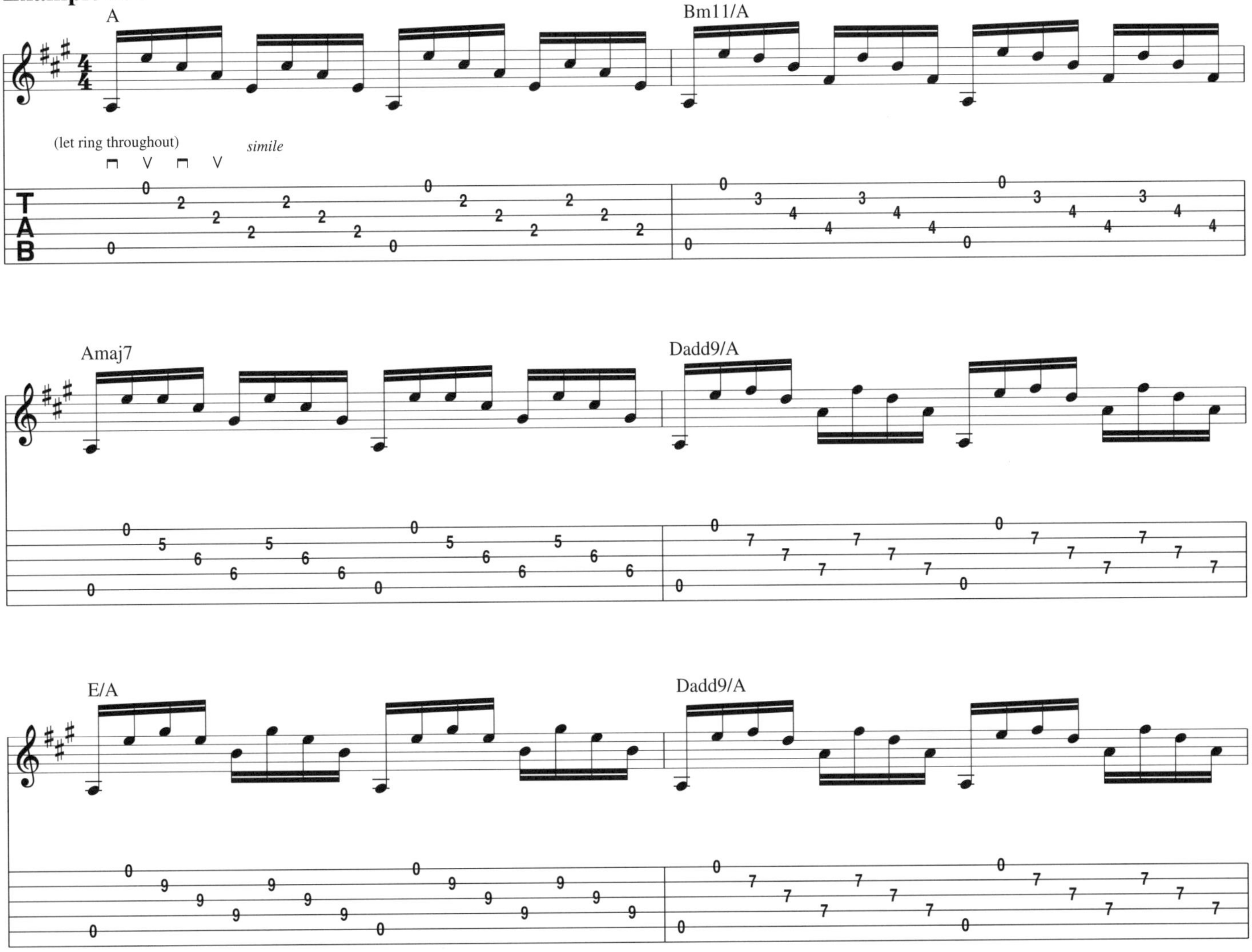

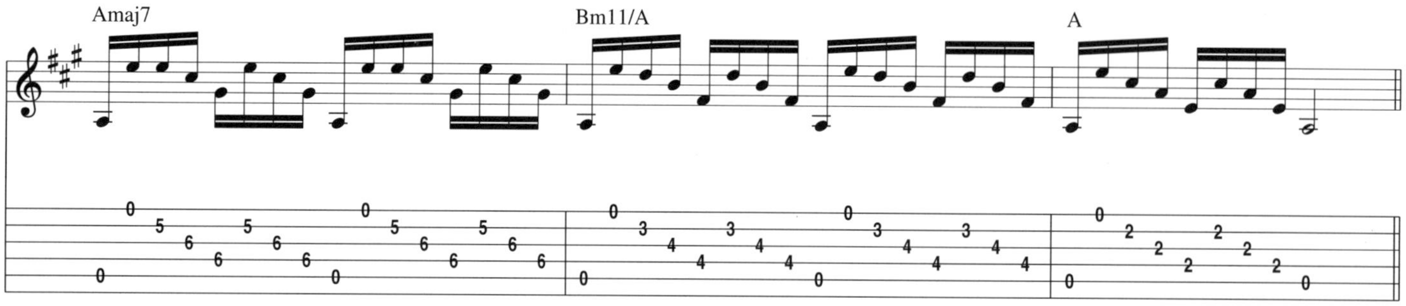

In the next set of examples, we will explore various sequences of the open position E major chord. Once again, watch your picking!

Example 105

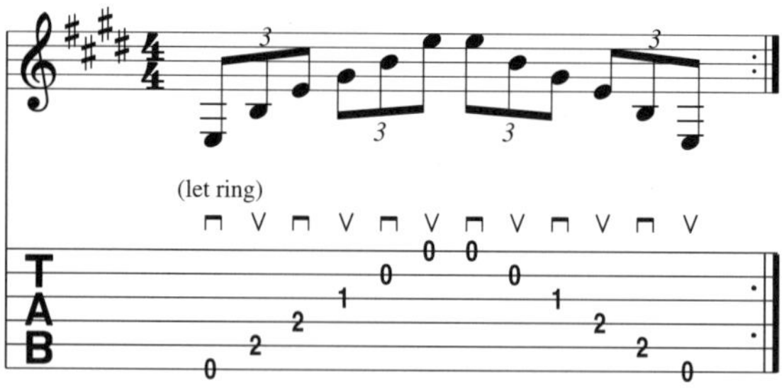

Example 106

Example 107

Example 108

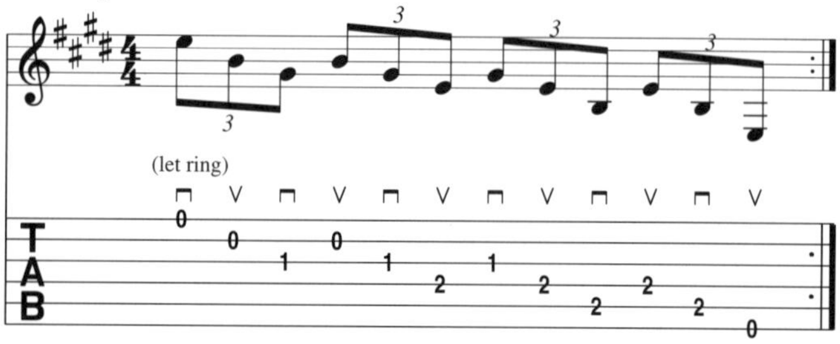

Example 109

Example 110

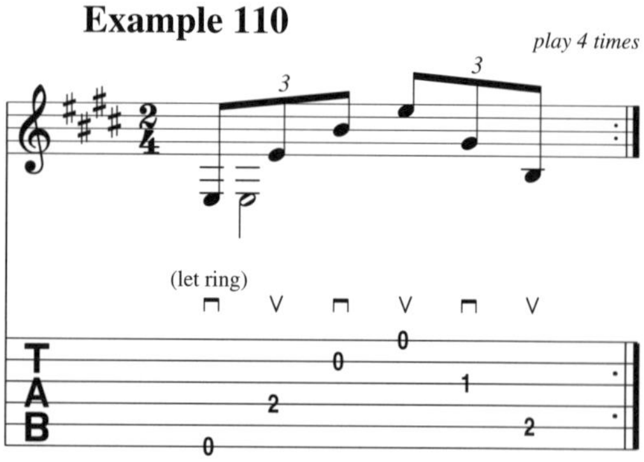

Example 111

Example 112

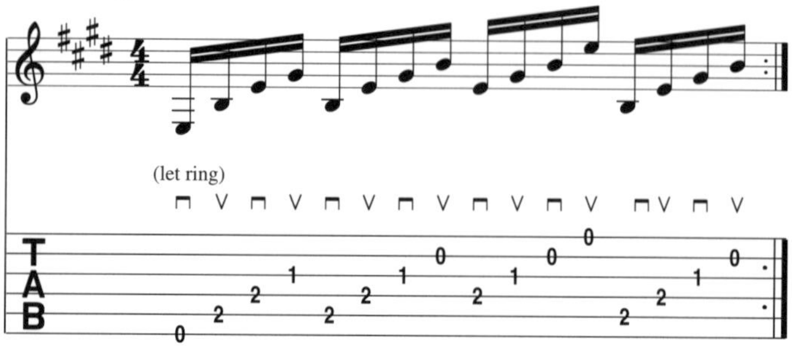

The following rythmic variations of the arpeggiated E chord will help you to increase the versatility of your alternate picking. Observe the picking instructions of each example closely.

Example 113

Example 114

Example 115

Example 116

Example 117

Single Note Arpeggiation

Up to this point, we've worked only with arpeggiation of basic chord shapes, allowing the notes to ring together harmonically. The exercises in this next section utilize shapes that lend themselves to the separation of the notes.

The following examples illustrate an effective method for gaining control of basic two-octave arpeggio shapes. This procedure of starting with a small part of the shape and adding one string at a time should be applied to all the basic triad arpeggios (see scale and arpeggio appendix).

9 Examples 118-138

Example 118

Example 119

Example 120

Example 121

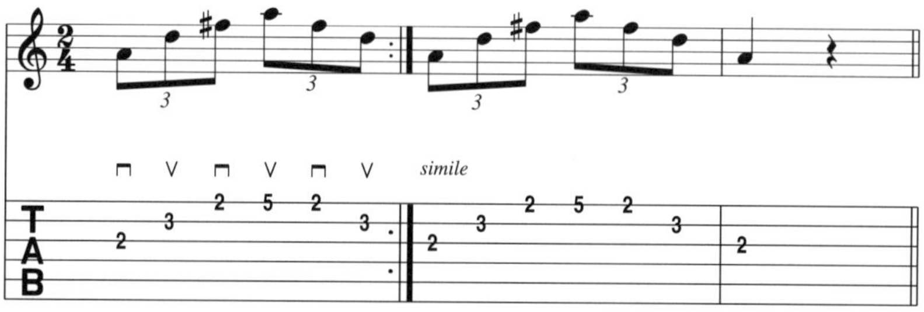

Example 122

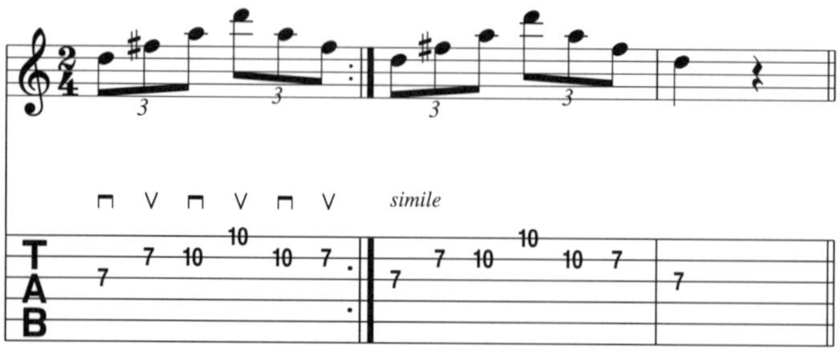

Example 123

Example 124

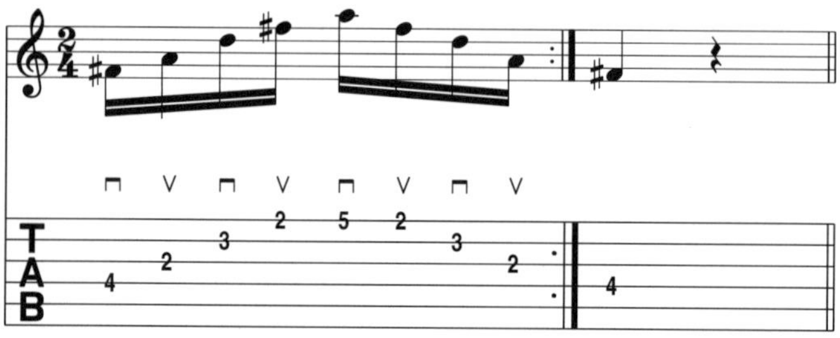

Example 125

Example 126

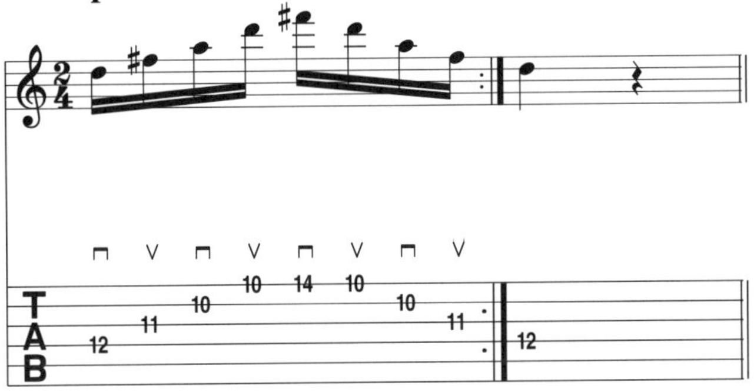

Example 127

Example 128

Example 129

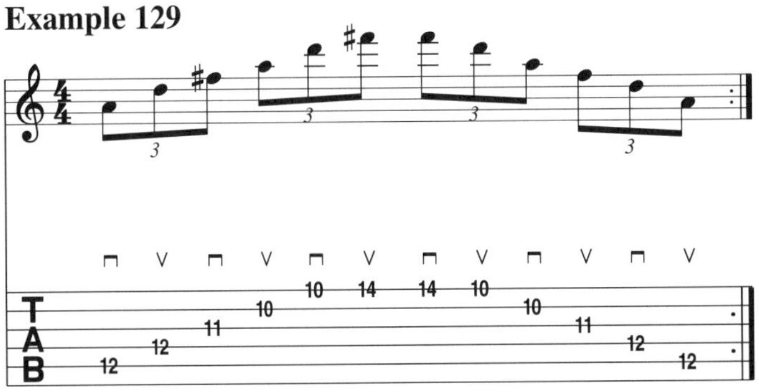

Just as we applied sequences to the block chord arpeggios, we can do the same with single note arpeggios. The following examples illustrate a few possibilities. Be very particular with the picking.

Example 130

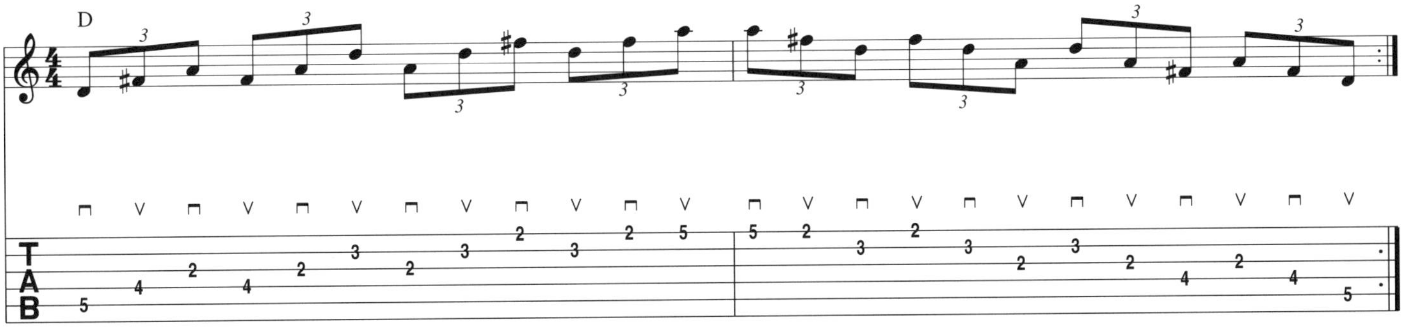

Example 131

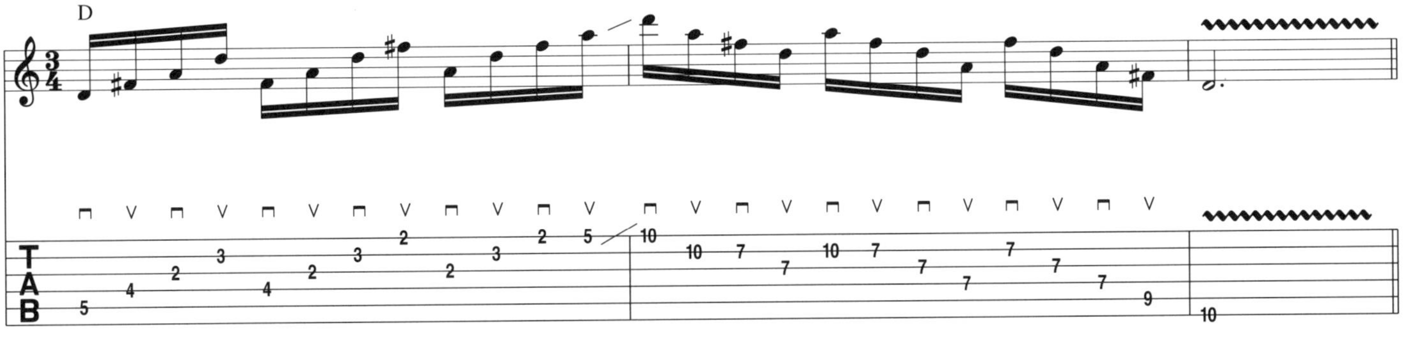

Example 132

In the next example, we will link a couple of arpeggio shapes together to create a new exercise. Work to gradually increase the tempo as you become comfortable with the picking.

Example 133

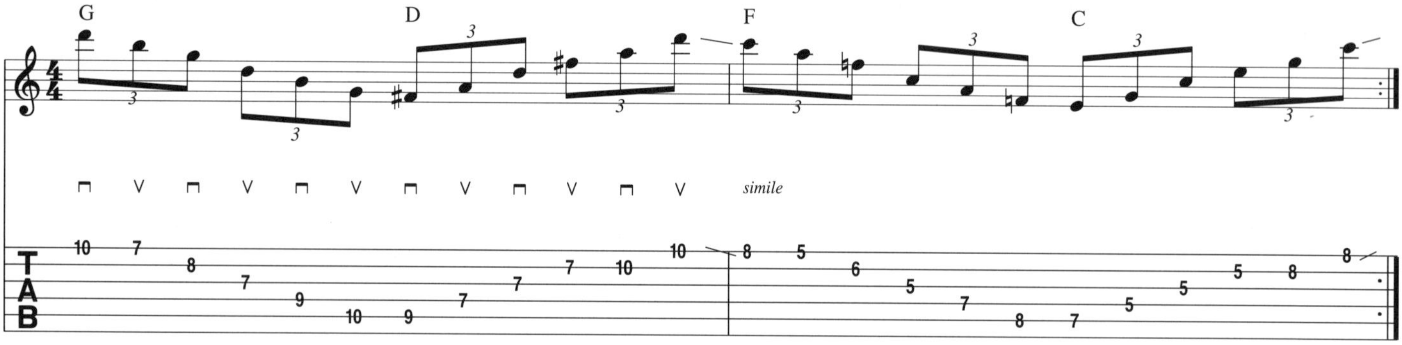

Here, diatonic arpeggios in the key of C are linked together in a lengthy line that travels most of the fretboard.

Example 134

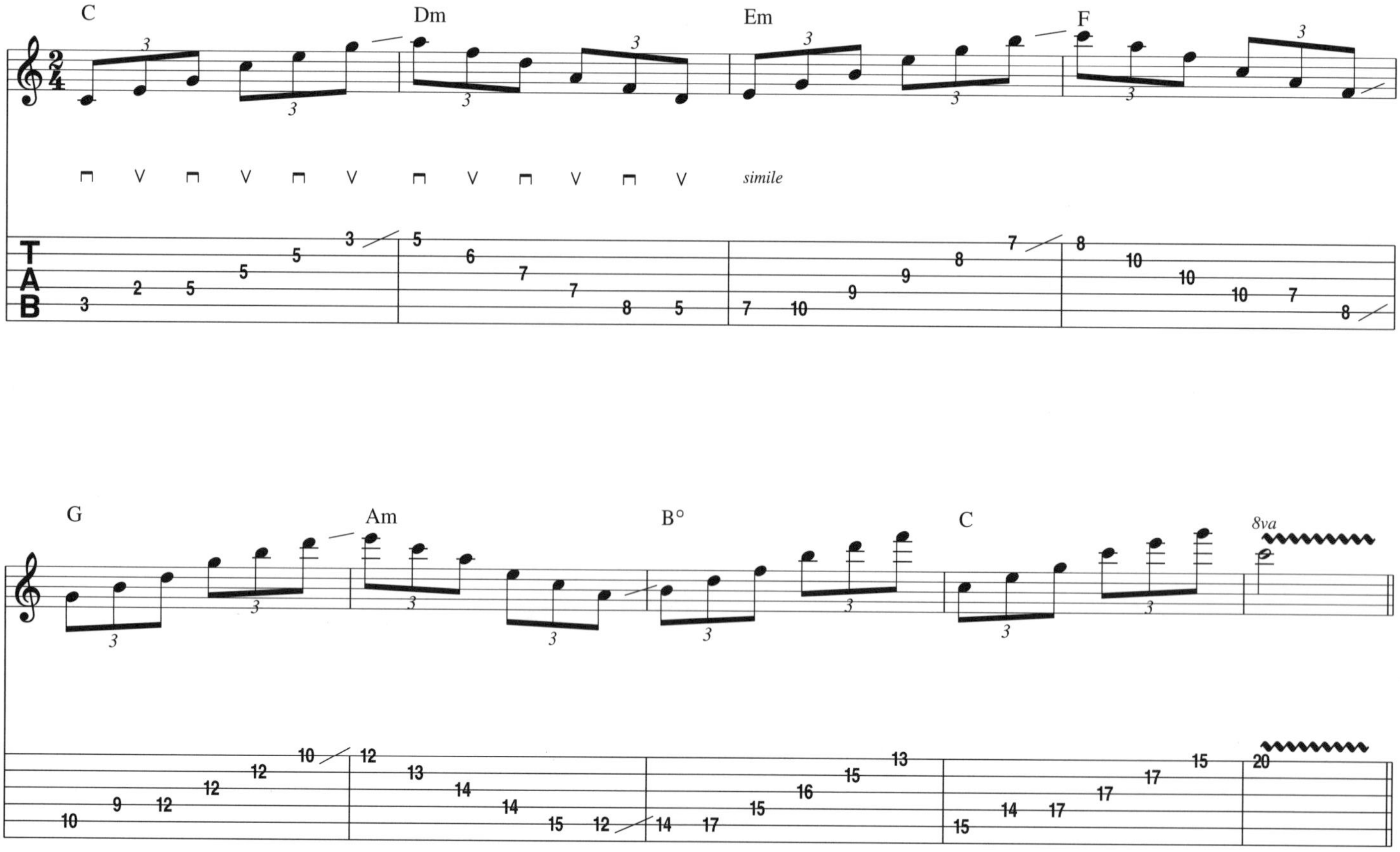

Arpeggios may be incorporated into positional sequences. These exercises are very effective for developing alternate picking as well as increasing your facility with scale positions.

Example 135

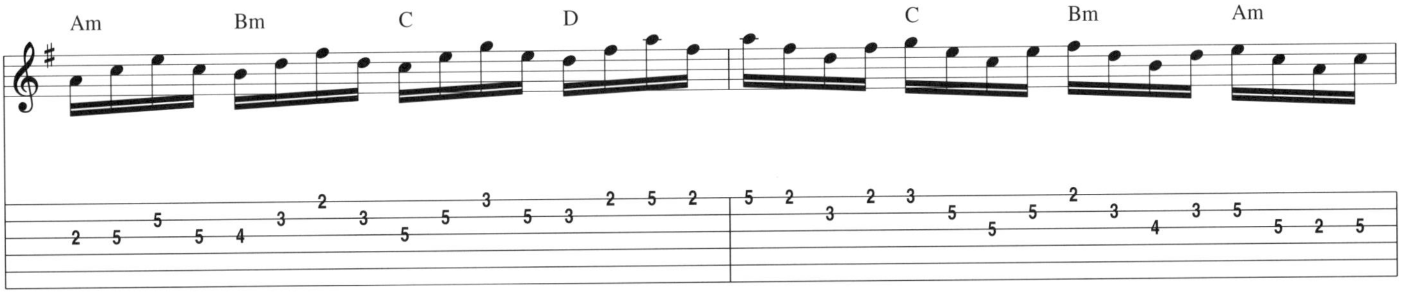

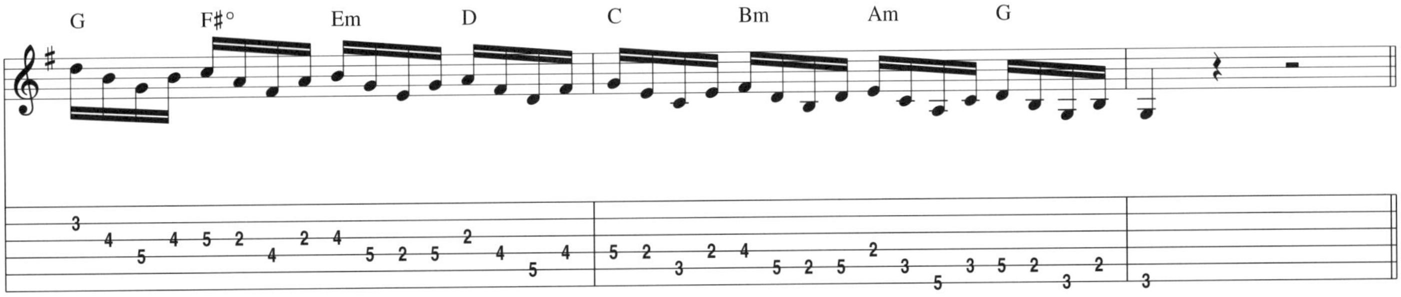

Example 136

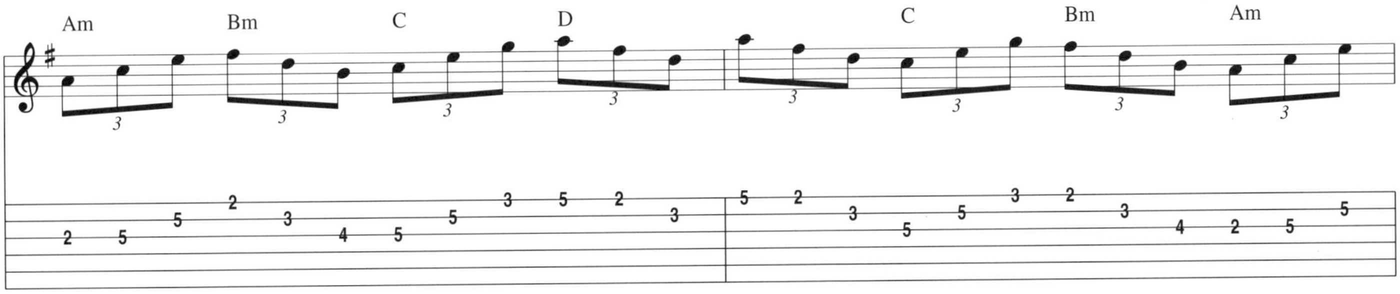

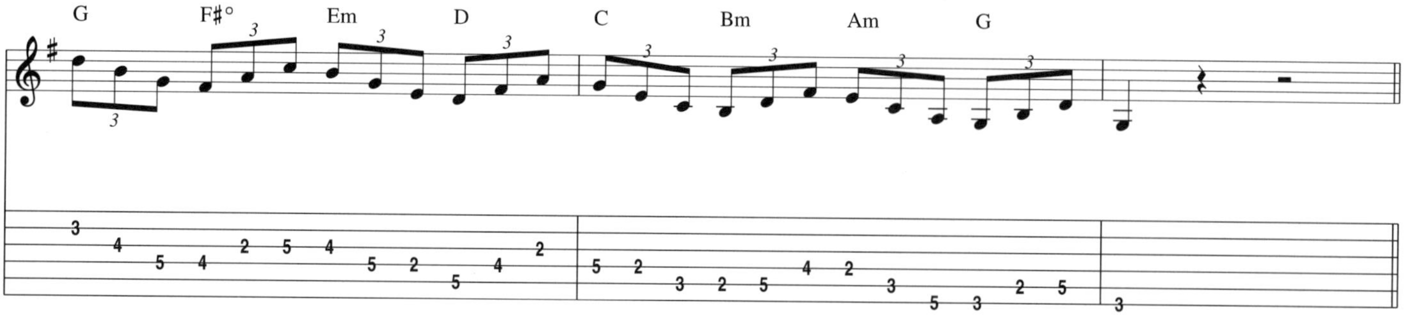
G
F♯°
Em
D
C
Bm
Am
G

Example 137

Gmaj7
N.C.
Am7
N.C.
Bm7
N.C.
Cmaj7
N.C.
simile
TAB
D7
N.C.
Em7
N.C.
F♯m7(♭5)
N.C.
Gmaj7
N.C.
Am7
N.C.
Bm7
N.C.
Bm7
N.C.
Am7
N.C.
Gmaj7
N.C.
F♯m7(♭5)
N.C.
Em7
N.C.
D7
N.C.

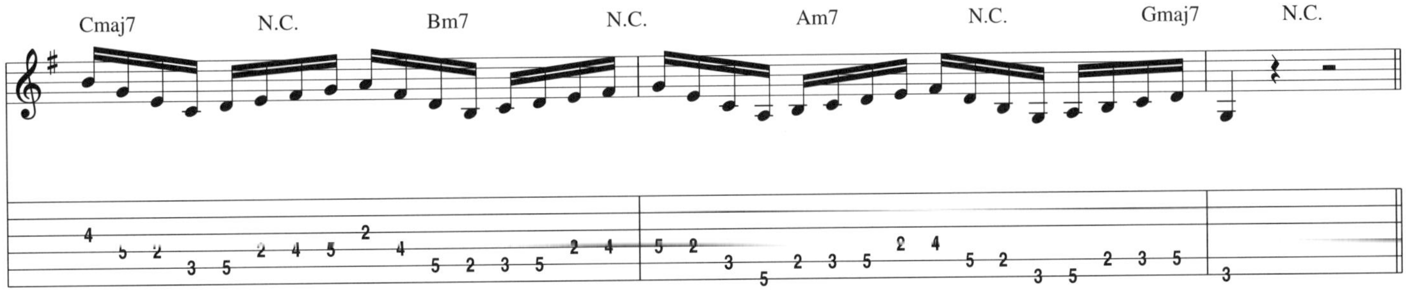

Once you've mastered the preceding positional arpeggio sequences as shown, try applying them to each of the remaining caged position major scale patterns (see appendix) in all twelve major keys. You'll be surprised at how easy it is to do this as your instinct and ears take over.

Here is an alternate picking arpeggio study. Once the study has been memorized, work with the metronome set at a tempo at which you can play through the entire line perfectly. Raise the tempo only when a level of ease has been established.

Example 138

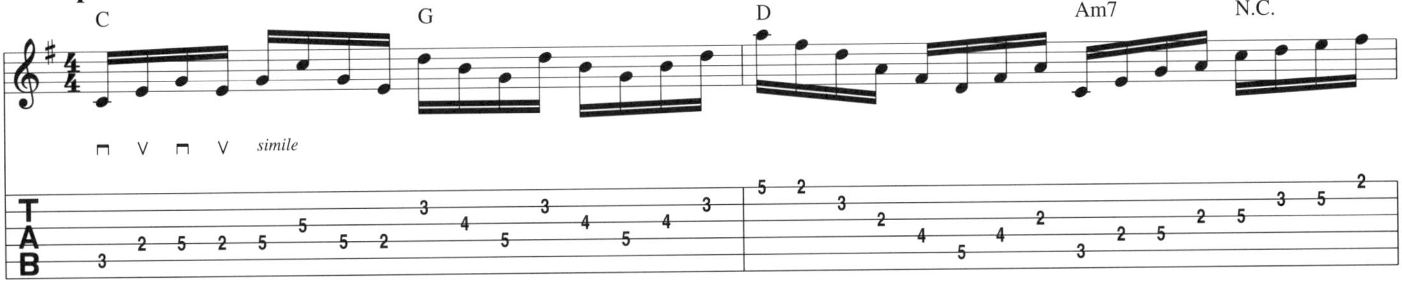

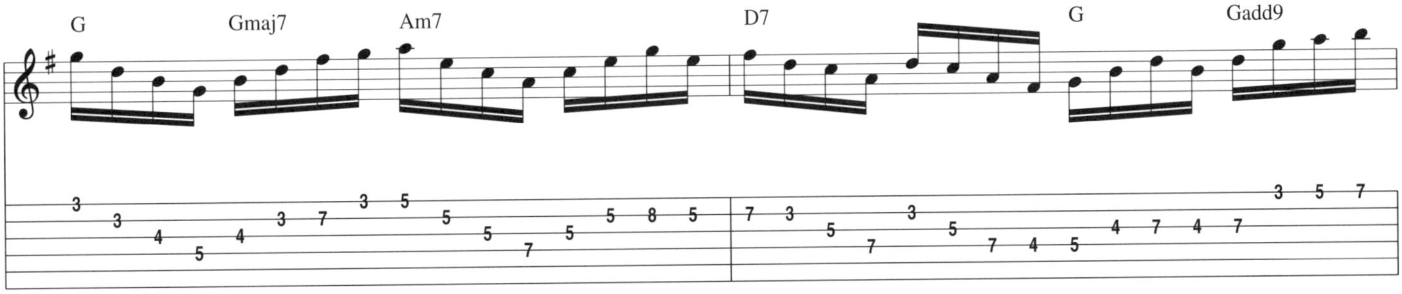

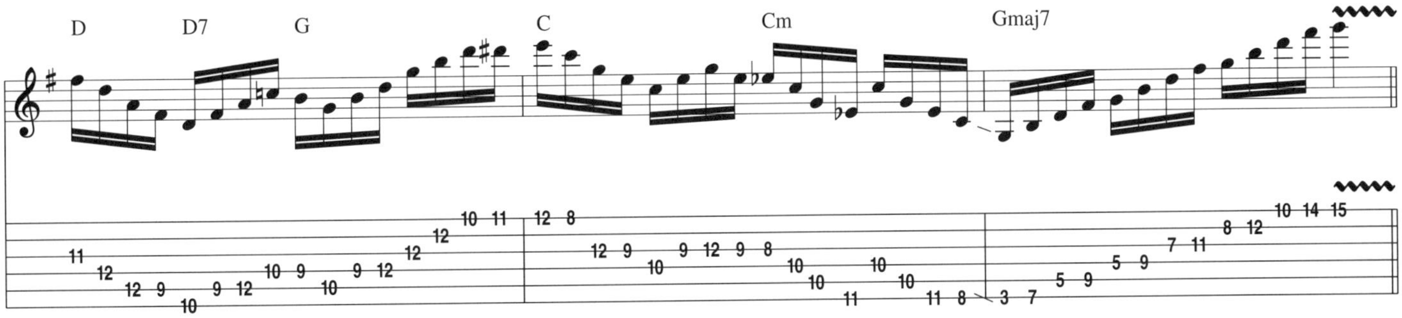

ECONOMY AND SWEEP PICKING

Basic Concepts

Although alternate picking is arguably the most versatile picking method, it may be beneficial to use economy picking on occasion for greater speed and fluidity. This technique incorporates successive downstrokes and upstrokes in order to travel across the strings with the least amount of right hand movement.

Economy picking can be most practically developed with arpeggios and intervallic material which involve one-note-per string situations. Take a look at the following simple minor arpeggios.

⑩ Example 139

Example 139A
Alternative picking

Example 139B
Economy or Sweep picking

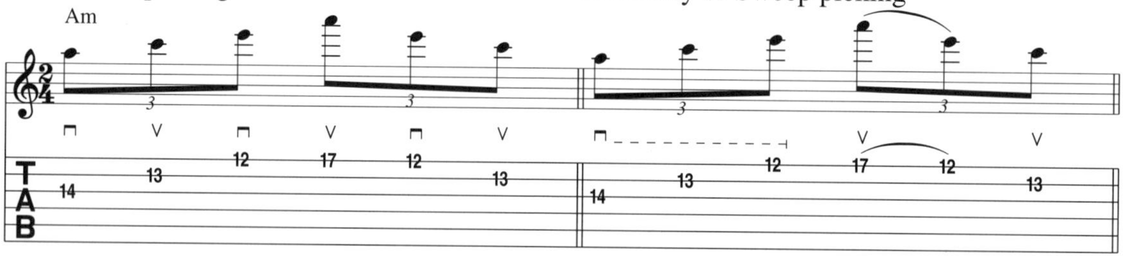

When making the downstroke in Example 139b, strive for one continuous "sweeping" motion as you cross the three strings, rather than three individual downstrokes. This is where the "economy" comes in. You'll find that this is much easier to practice at a medium tempo than a slow one. However, as you raise the tempo it becomes very easy to lose the rhythmic definition. Practice with a metronome, and remember that cleaner chops are much more effective than blurry ones.

Arpeggios

Now, let's take a look at the application of this technique to a larger arpeggio shape. When taking on a two octave arpeggio, it is best to first separate the ascending and descending strokes (a & b), then connect them for one continuous line (c).

⑪ Examples 140-167

Example 140A

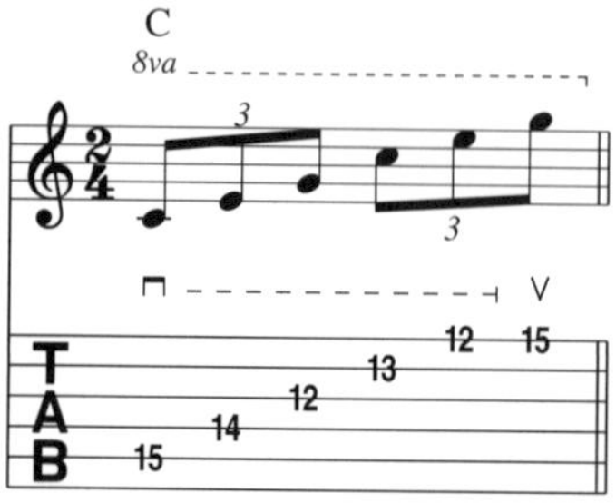

Example 140B

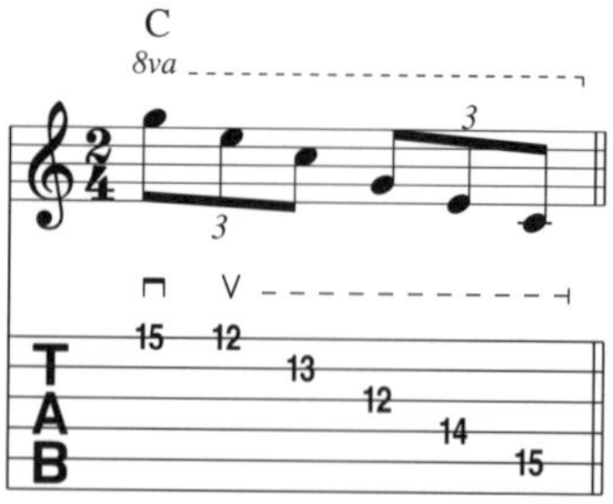

Example 140C

Further possibilities with the basic arpeggio shape from Example 140 can be discovered by breaking it down into smaller patterns. The following set of examples start with the smallest components and work up to gradually combine those components together.

Example 141

Example 142

Example 143

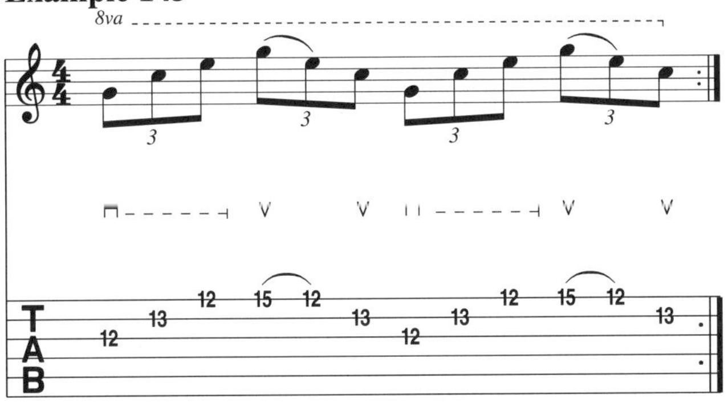

Example 144

Example 145

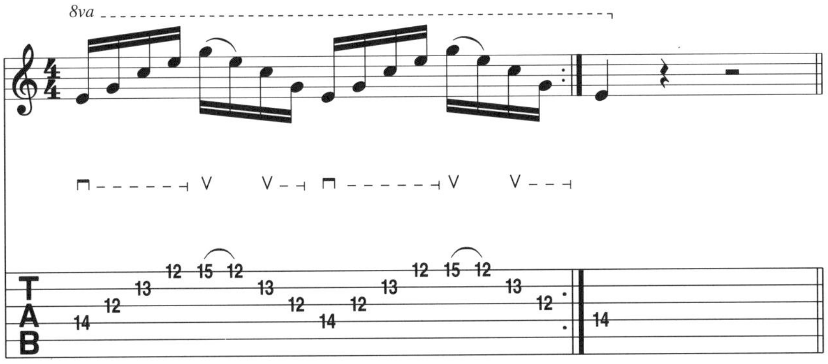

Example 146

Example 147

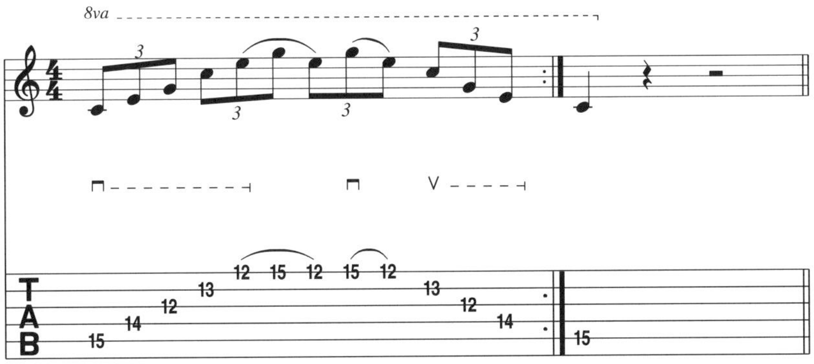

Example 148

Use the methodical approach for developing the sweep picking technique shown on the previous page when working on the following examples.

Example 149

Example 150

Example 151

Example 152

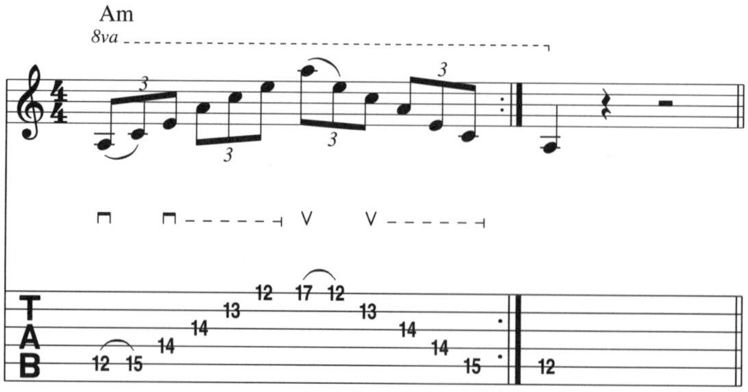

Example 153

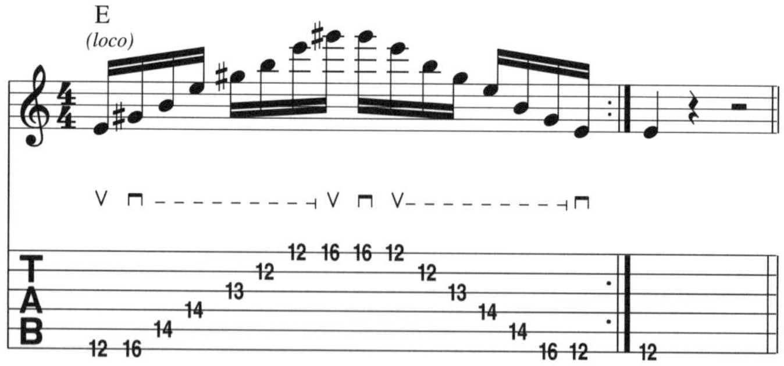

Example 154

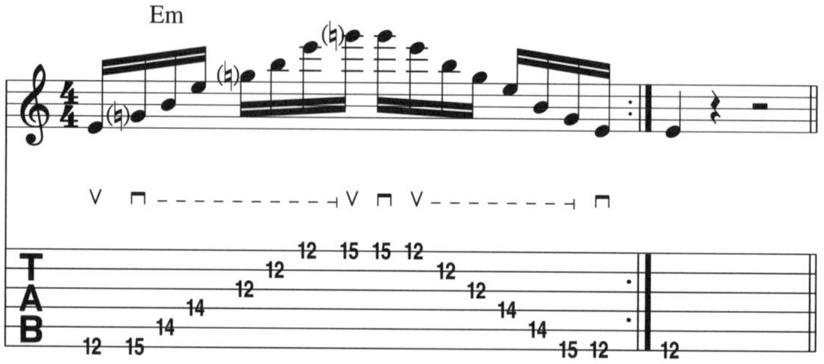

Example 155

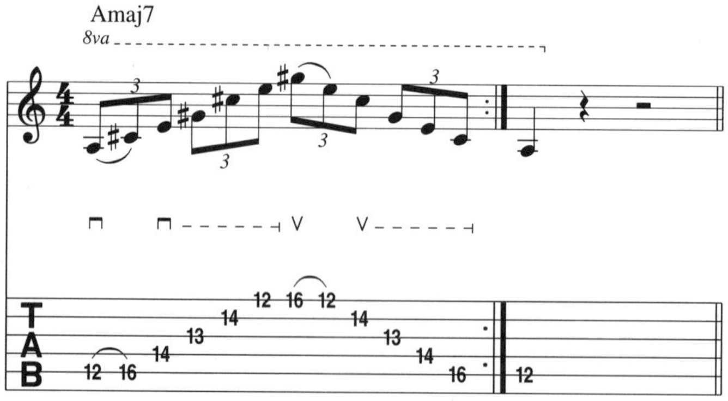

Example 156

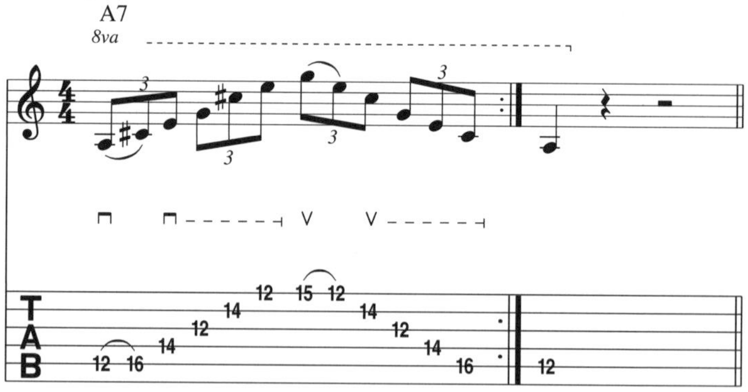

Example 157

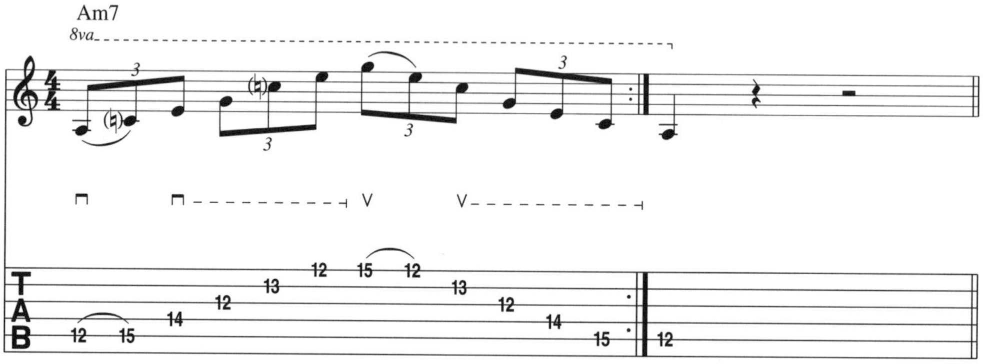

The following sweep picking study utilizes some of the shapes we've studied along with one new one, the diminished 7th (notice the similarity to the dominant 7th). This example uses the same picking pattern throughout. Strive for rhythmic accuracy.

Example 158

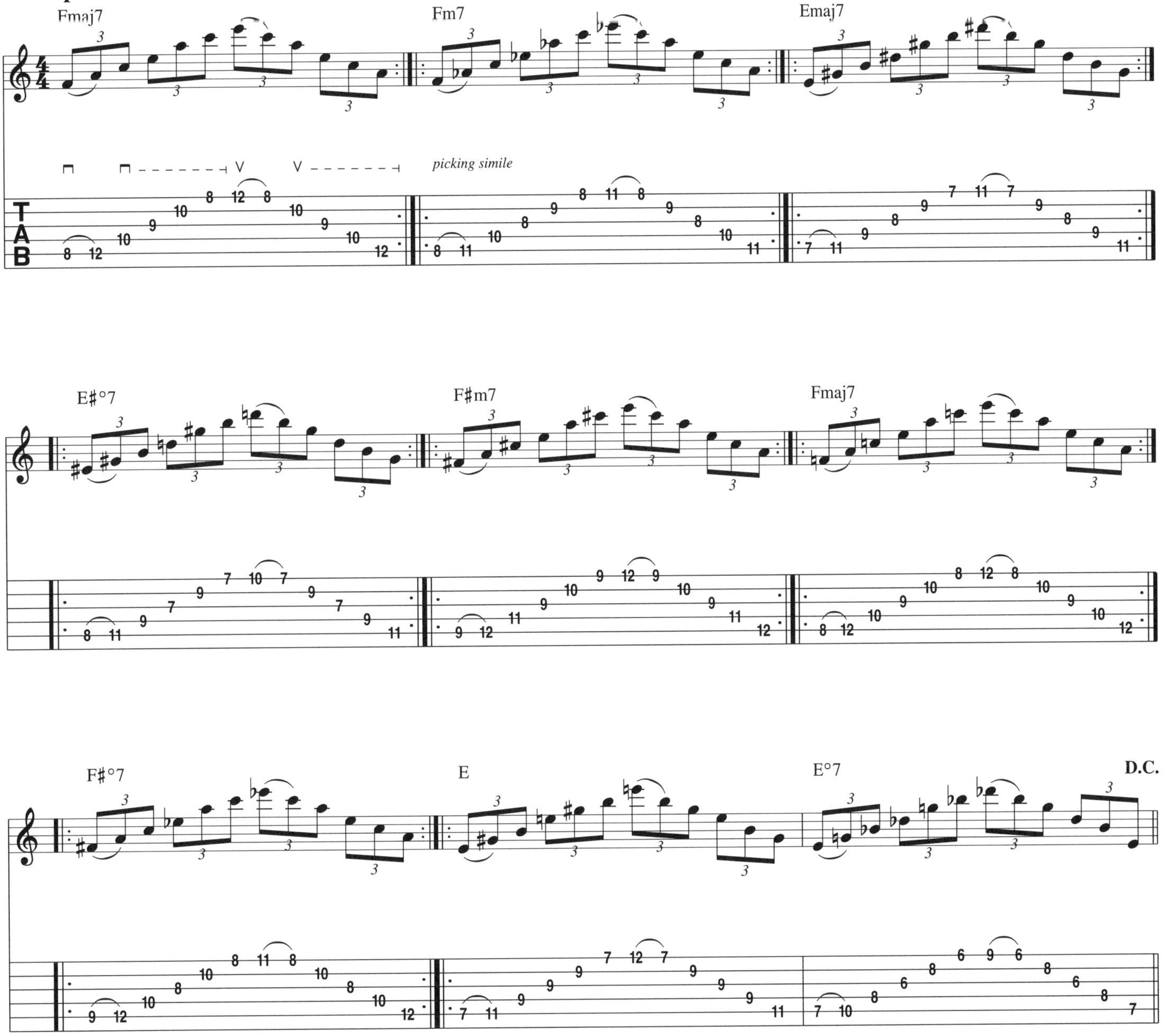

The following modal arpeggio shapes can help you combine economy picking with alternate picking. Take special care with the notes on the fourth string. The transition between positions should be as smooth as possible.

Example 159

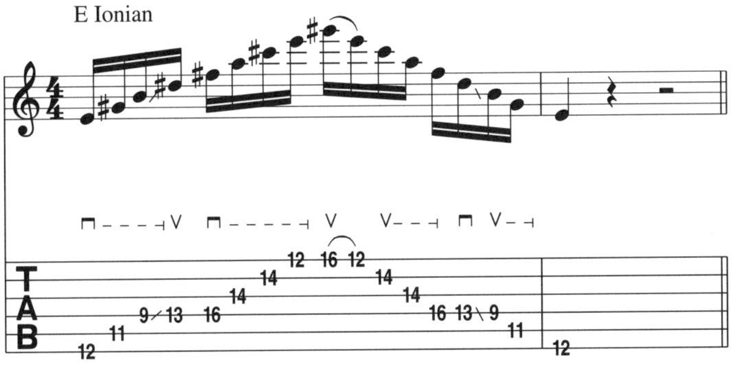

Example 160

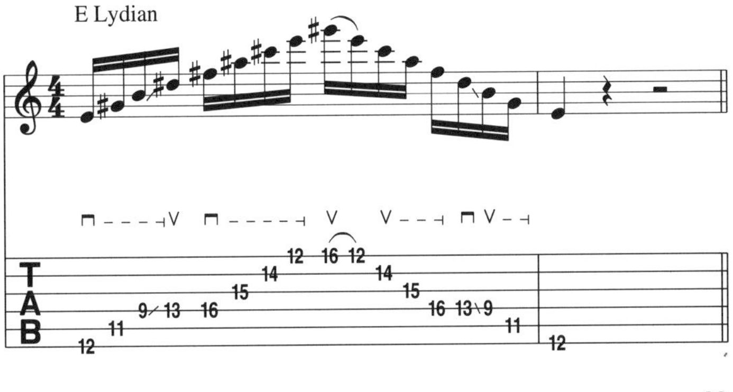

Example 161

E Mixolydian

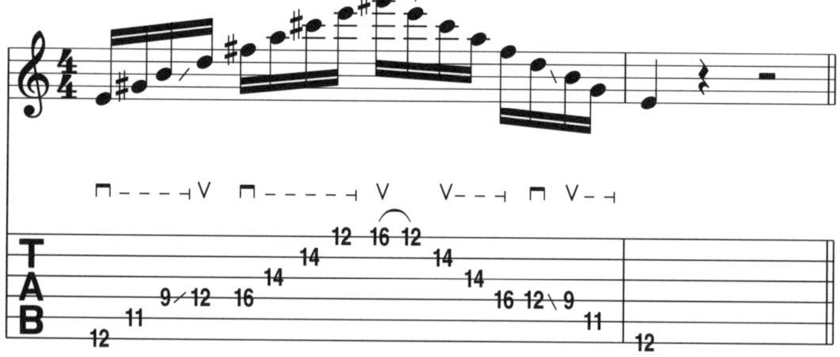

Example 162

E Phrygian Dominant

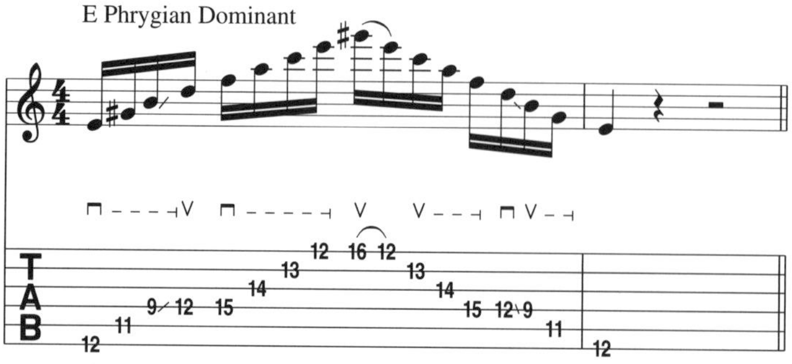

Example 163

E Aeolian

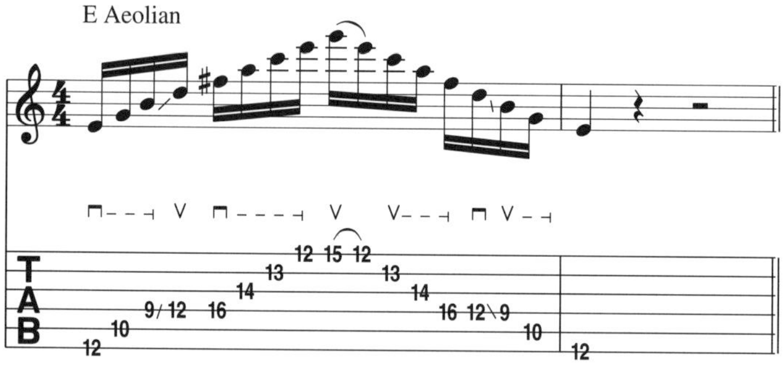

Example 164

E Dorian

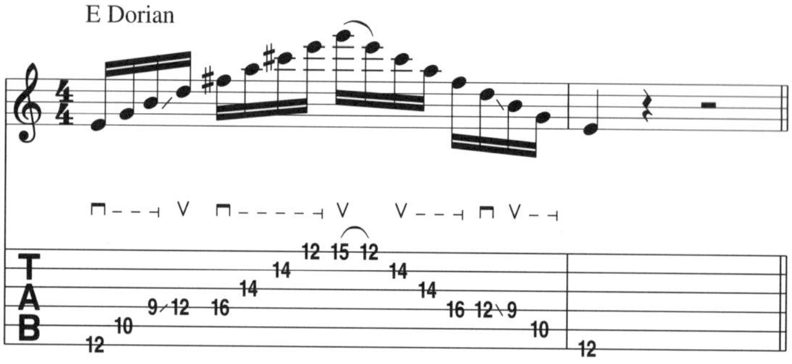

Example 165

E Phrygian

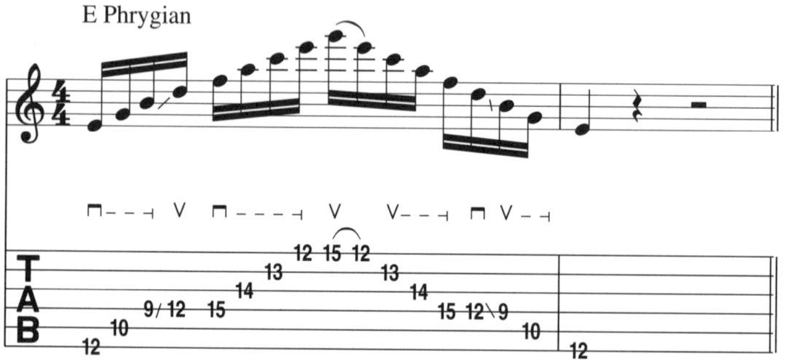

Example 166

E Locrian

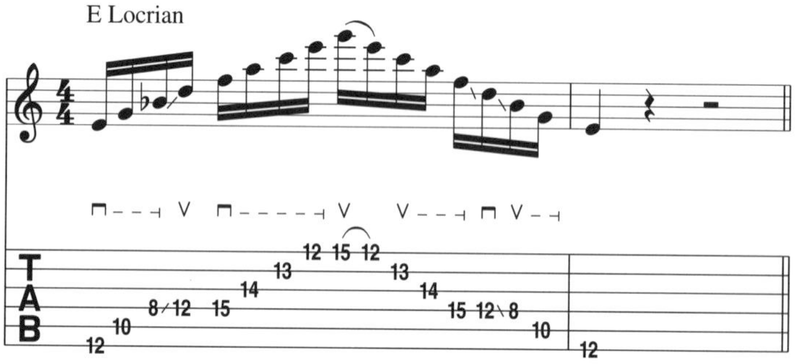

Although the economy picking study shown below incorporates the small one octave arpeggio sequence throughout, the line can be quite difficult to master. Have fun!

Example 167

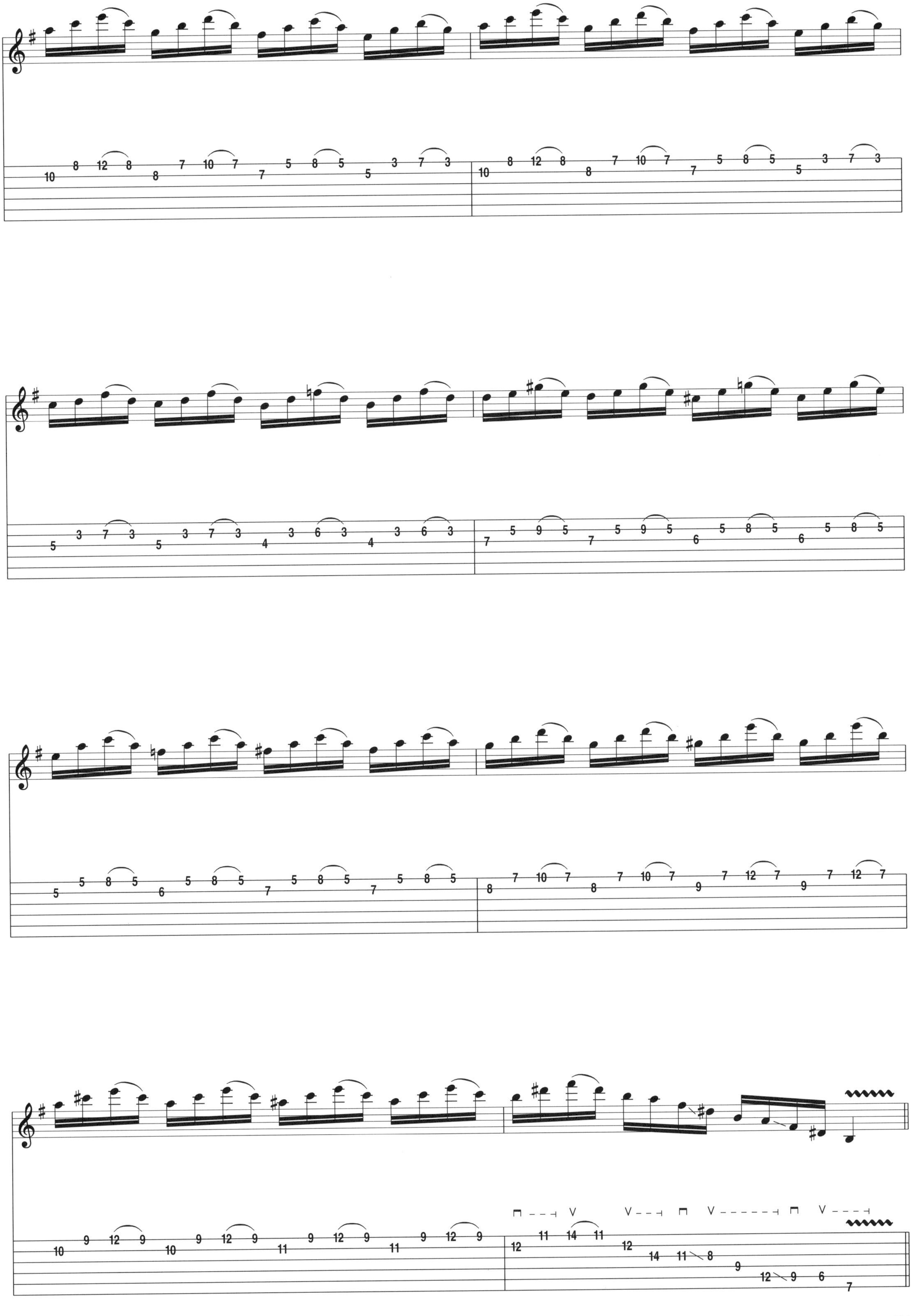

HYBRID PICKING

Basic Concepts

Another picking technique that deserves our attention is that of "hybrid picking" (often called "chicken pickin'" in country music circles). This technique incorporates the pick along with one or more right hand fingers, resulting in a hybrid of pickstyle and fingerstyle.

The quickest way to get a handle on hybrid picking is to try applying it to common phrases, such as the following minor pentatonic phrases.

⊓ = downstroke with pick. m = medio, or middle finger.

V = upstroke with pick. a = anular, or ring finger.

12 Examples 168-176

Example 168

Example 169

These examples will help you develop rapid alternation of downstrokes and middle finger strokes.

Example 170

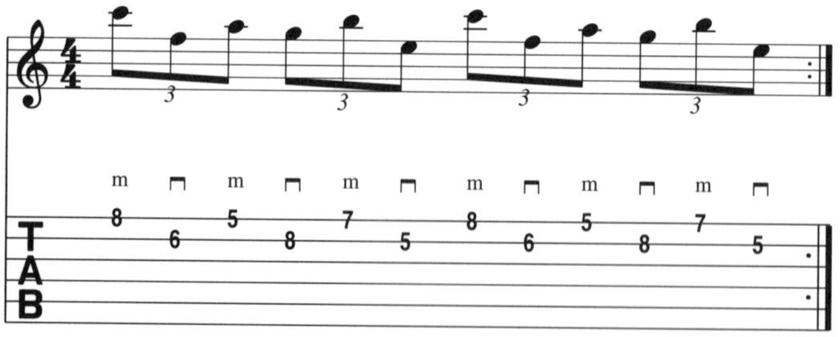

Example 171

Notice the simultaneous use of the middle and ring fingers as well as alternate picking in these country guitar phrases.

Example 172

Example 173

Hybrid picking can also be quite helpful on pivoting arpeggio lines, also knows as pedal-point in classical music.

Example 174

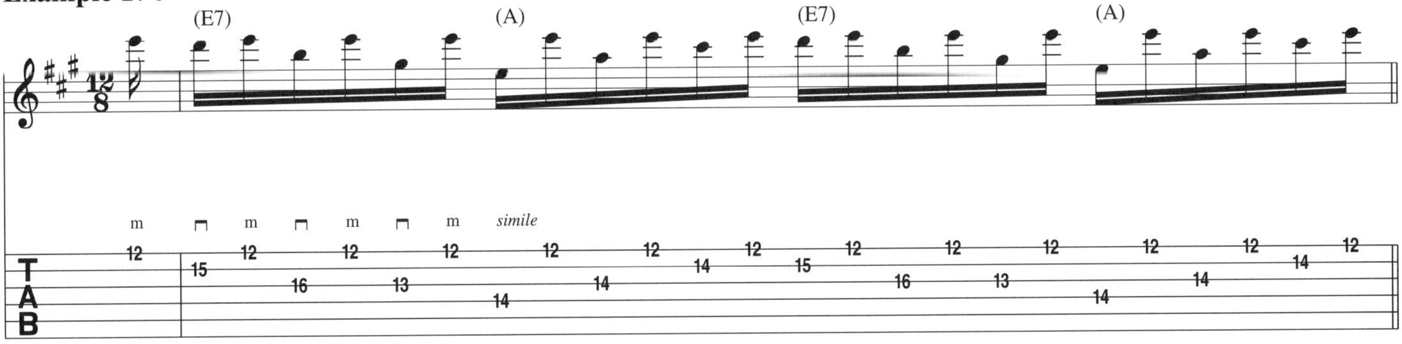

Example 175

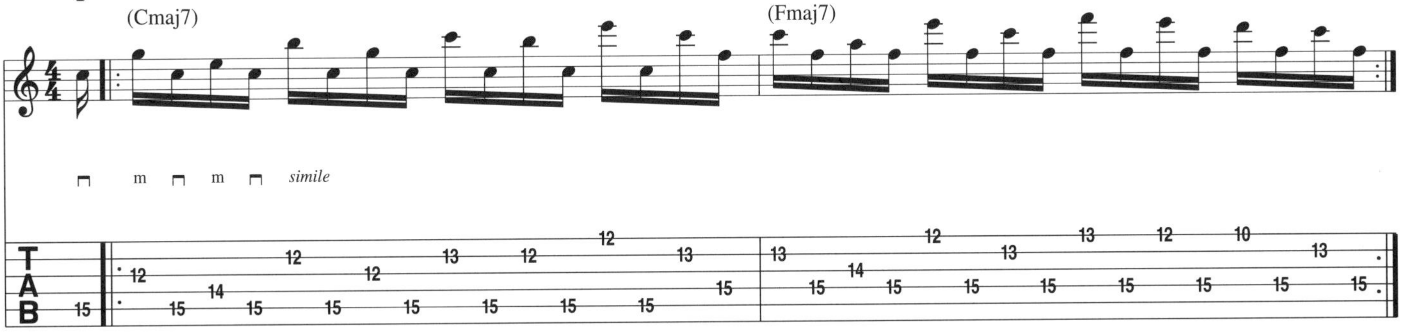

Hybrid picking may be used in scalar sequences as well as arpeggios. The following examples show the application of hybrid picking to ascending and descending scalar sequences in 6ths.

Example 176A Ascending C major scale

Example 176B Descending C major scale

LEGATO

Chromatic Exercises

Effective legato playing (hammer-ons and pull-offs) requires left hand strength and stamina. The following chromatic exercises will help you develop these skills. Each sequence is shown in ascending and descending versions and should be moved up chromatically to the 12th position before transferring to the next string and coming back down.

13 Examples 177-182

Example 177

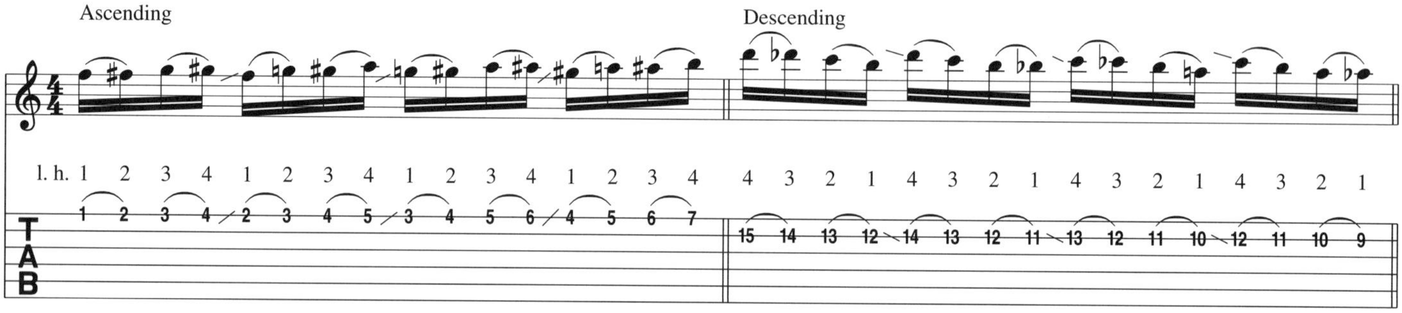

Example 178

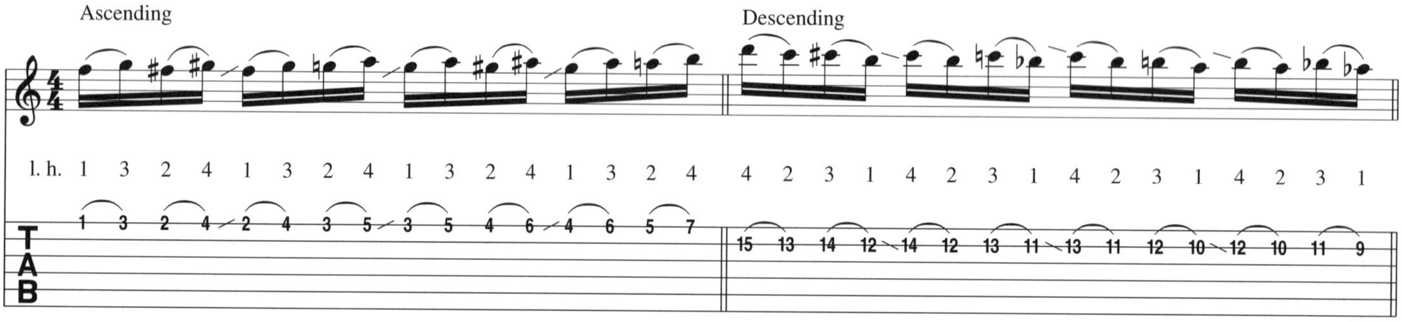

Example 179

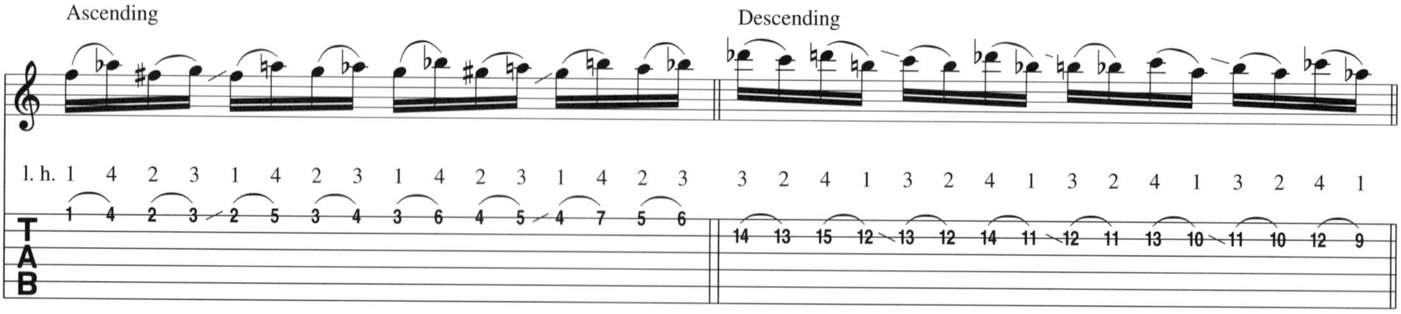

Example 180

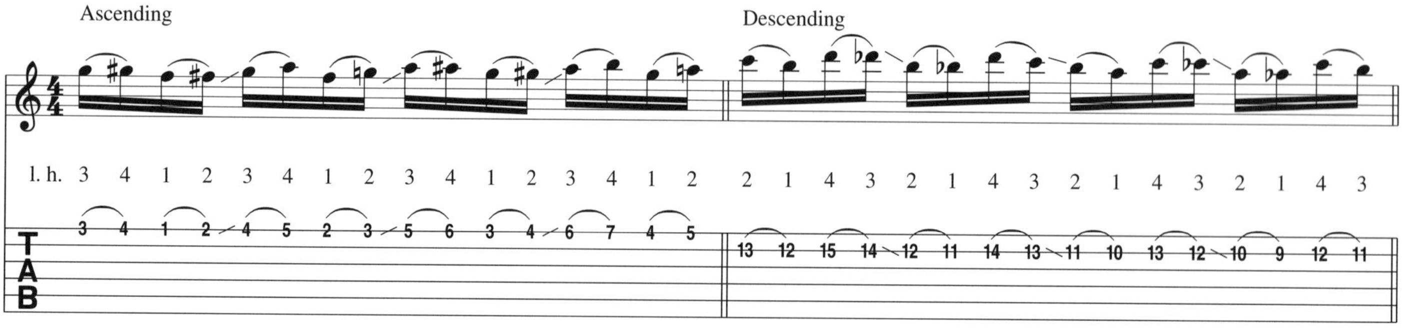

Example 181

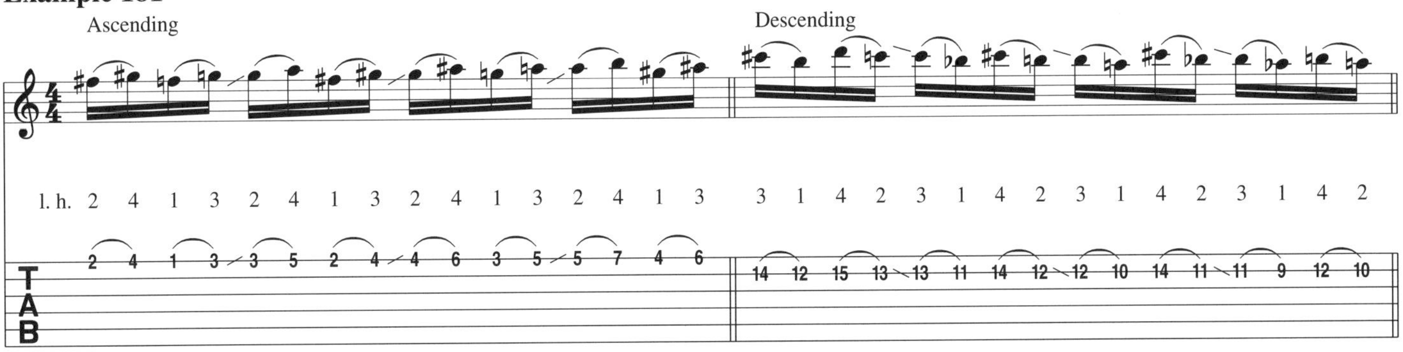

Example 182

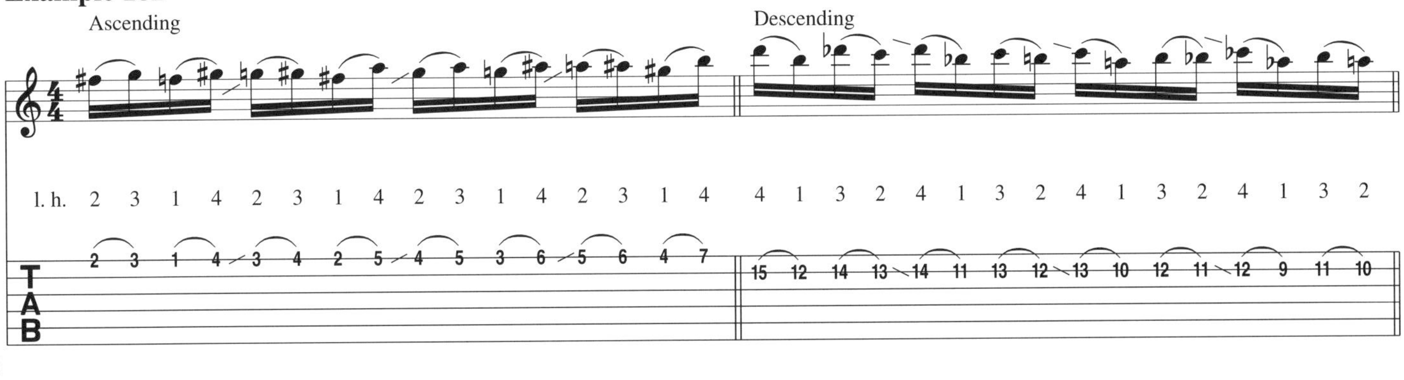

Scalar Sequences

Now, let's apply the legato technique to a major scale. Each of the following examples should be played through all seven three-note per string major scale patterns.

14 Examples 183-186

Example 183 Hammer-ons

Example 184 Pull-offs

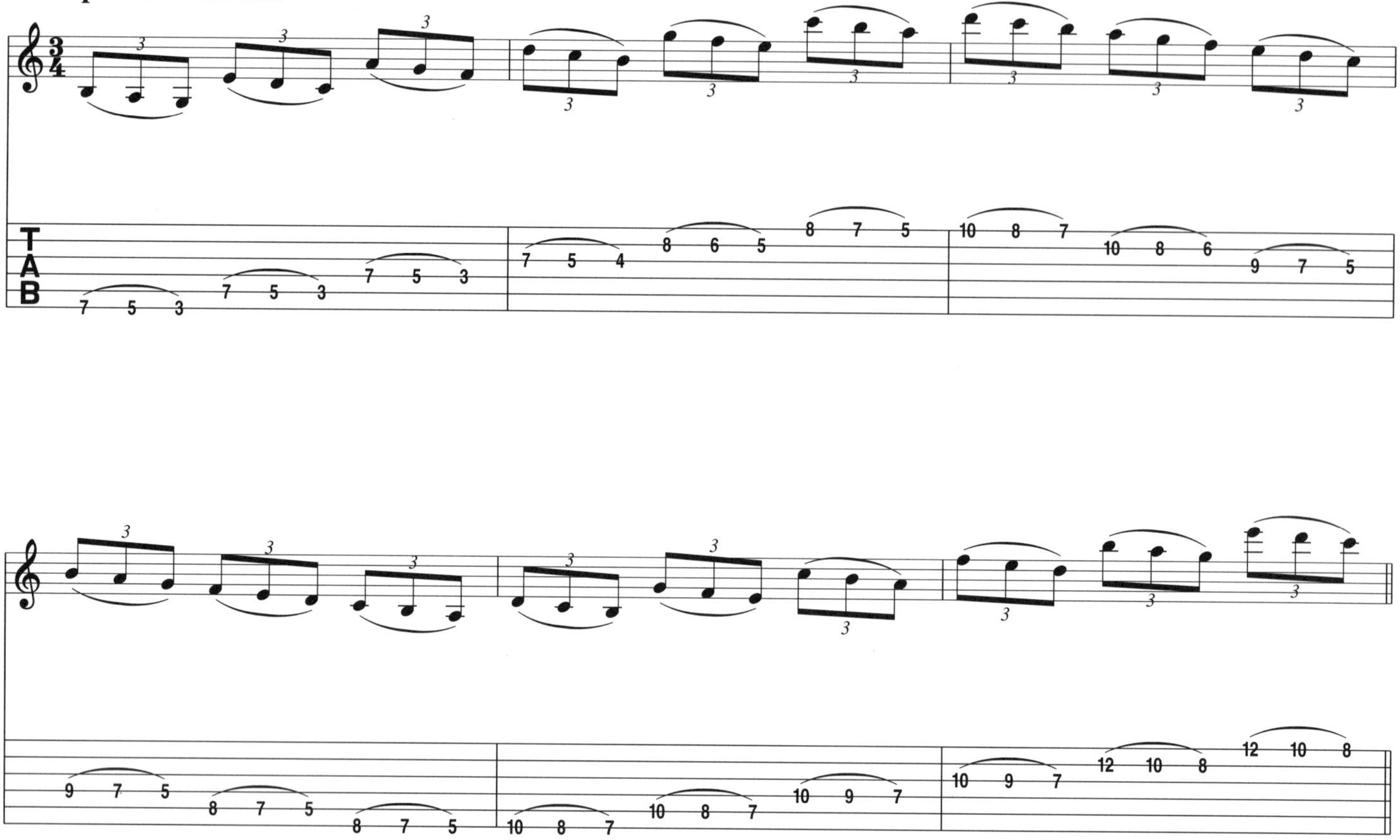

Here, we will incorporate combined hammer-ons and pull-offs with sequences we've seen earlier in the alternate picking section.

Example 185

Example 186

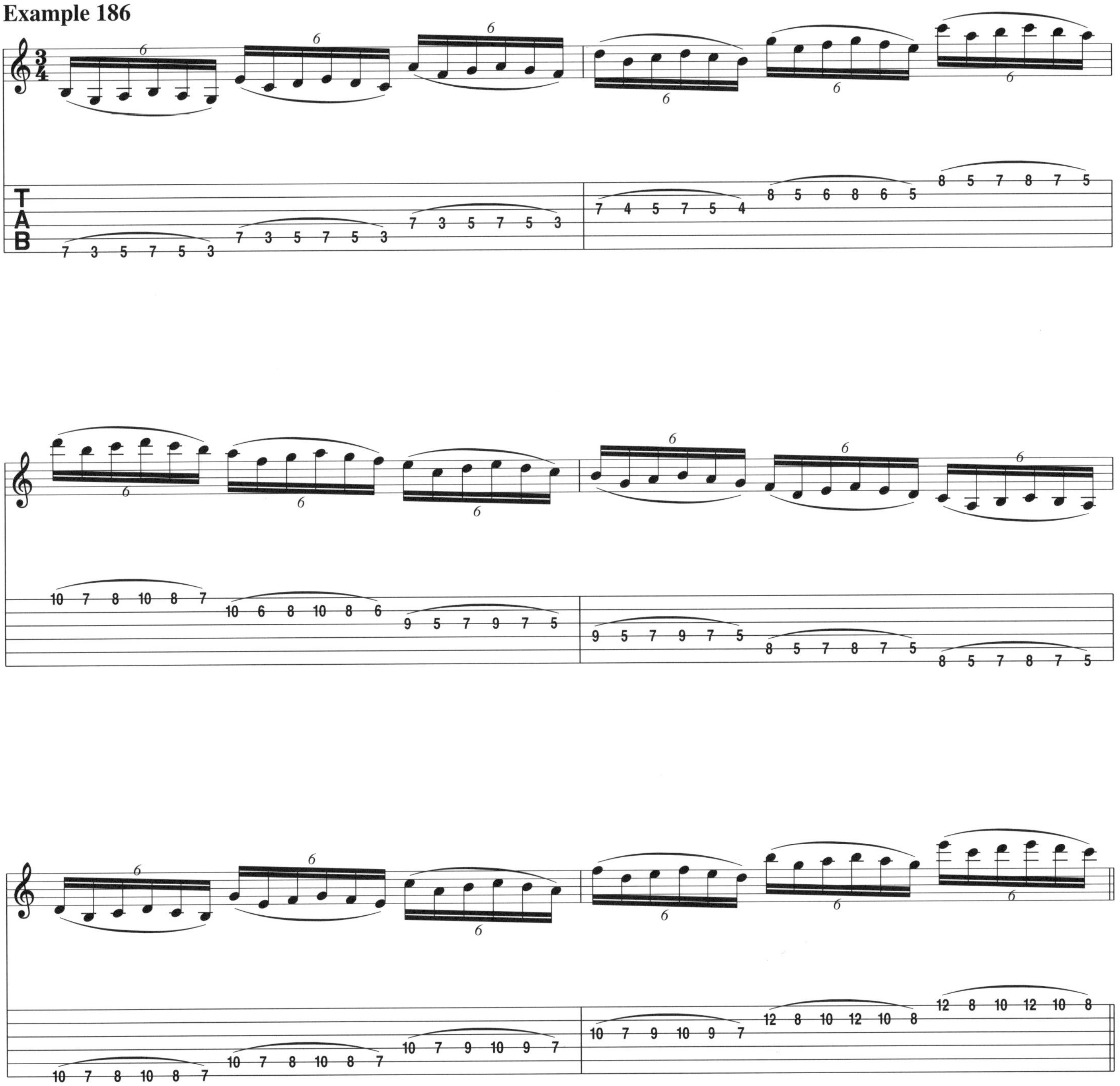

One-Handed Arpeggios

Most often, the hammer-on is not as strong a way to sound a note as the pull-off. The following examples utilize the hammer-on almost exclusively and can be of great help in facilitating its development. Notice that each of the examples is derived from simple arpeggio shapes. This type of work can be strenuous for the left hand, so don't overdo it.

Try muffling the strings behind the left hand with a rag or foam. I suggest using a smooth overdrive to help you achieve a fluid attack.

15 Examples 187-195

Example 187

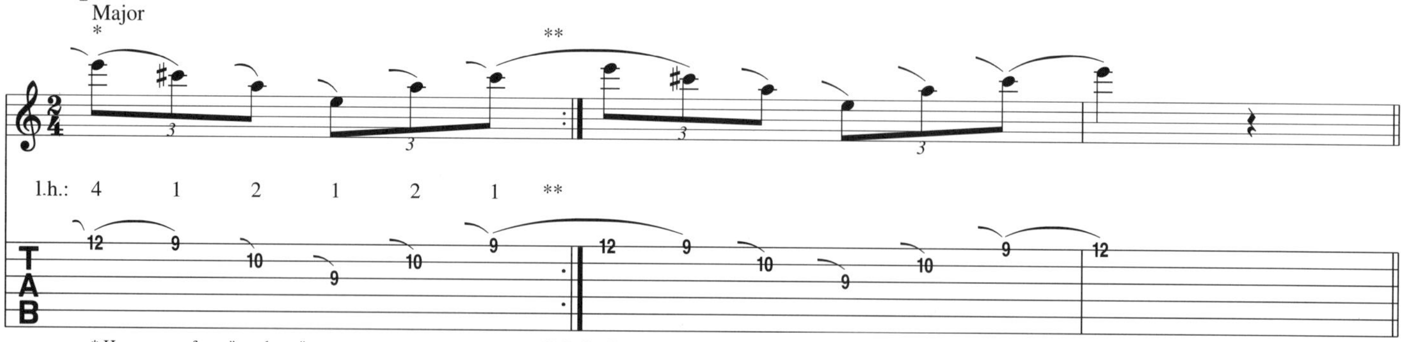

* Hammer-on from "nowhere." ** Pull off to first note on repeat.

Example 188

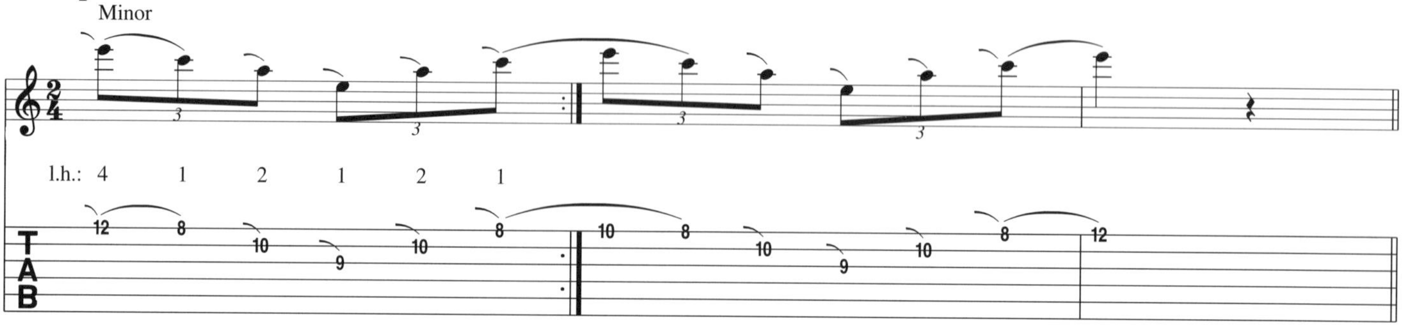

Example 189

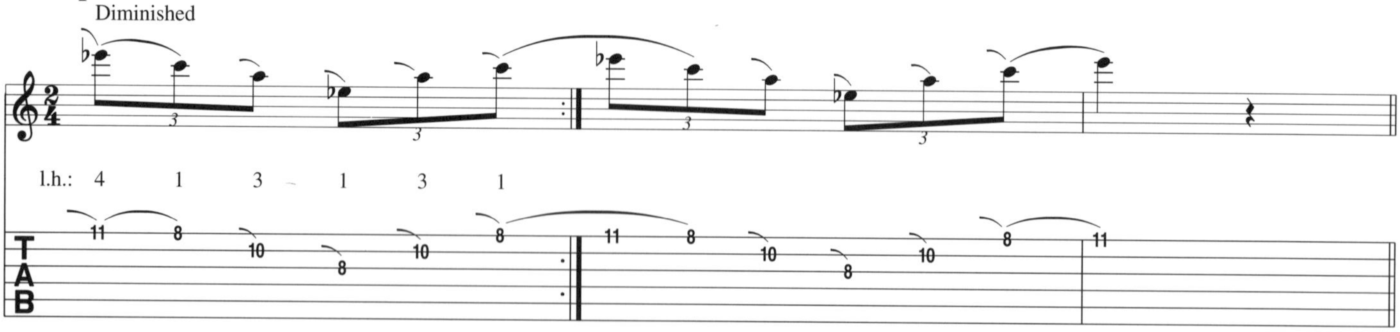

Example 190

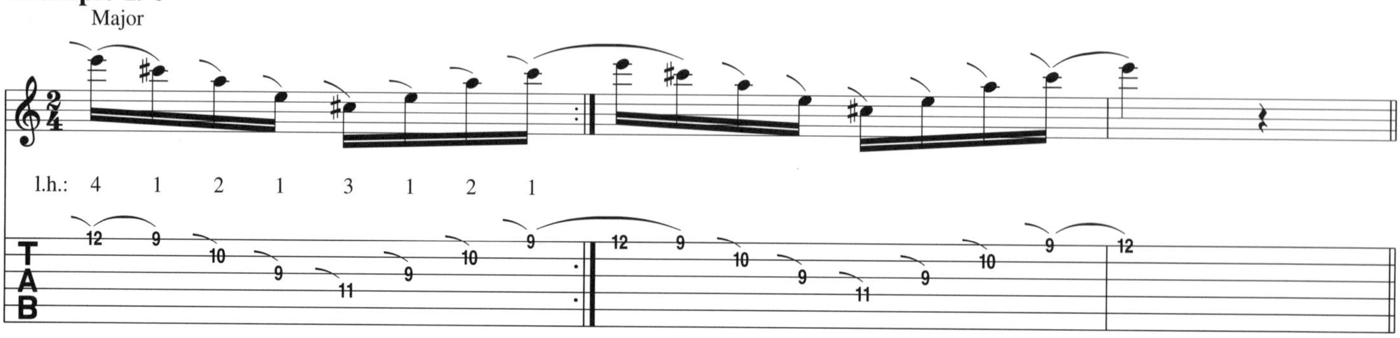

Example 191

Minor

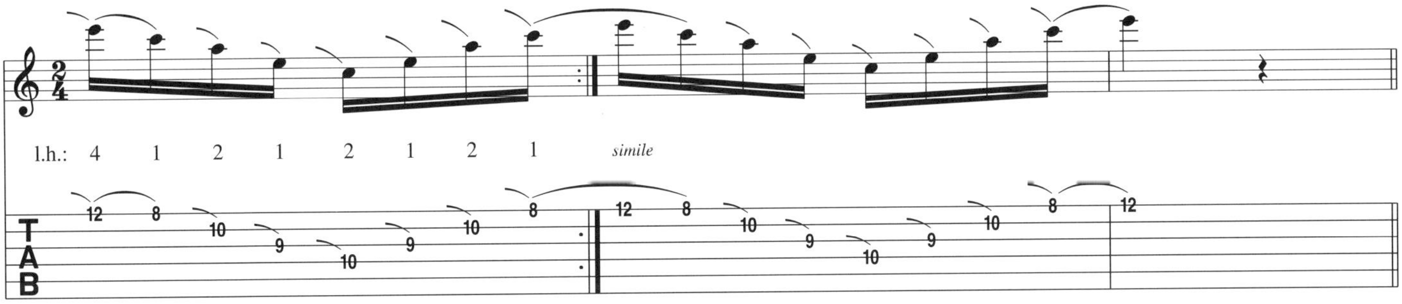

Example 192

Diminished

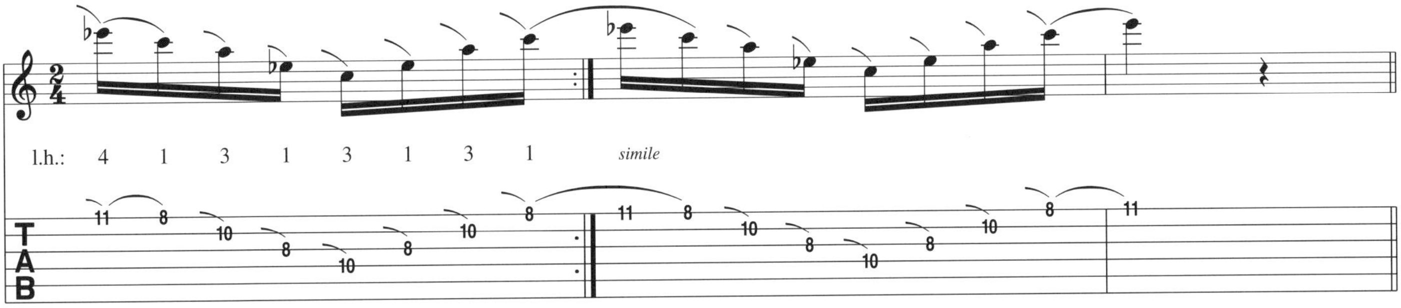

Example 193

Major

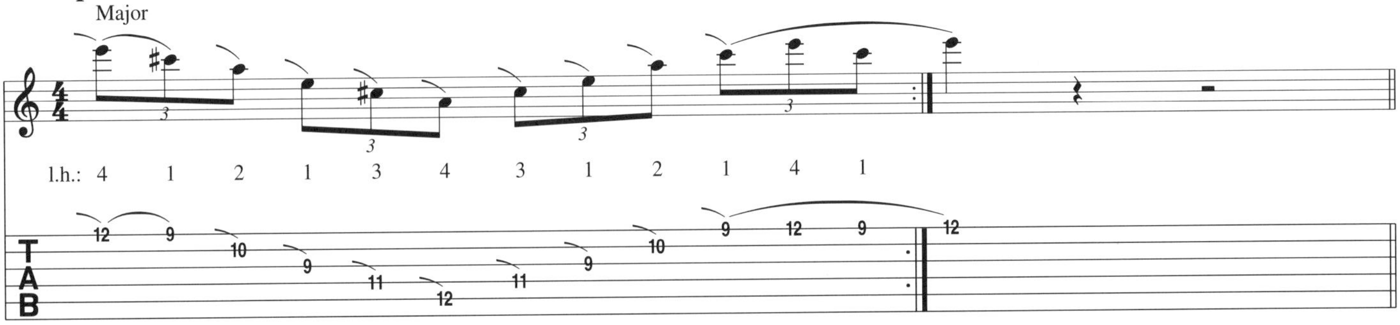

Example 194

Minor

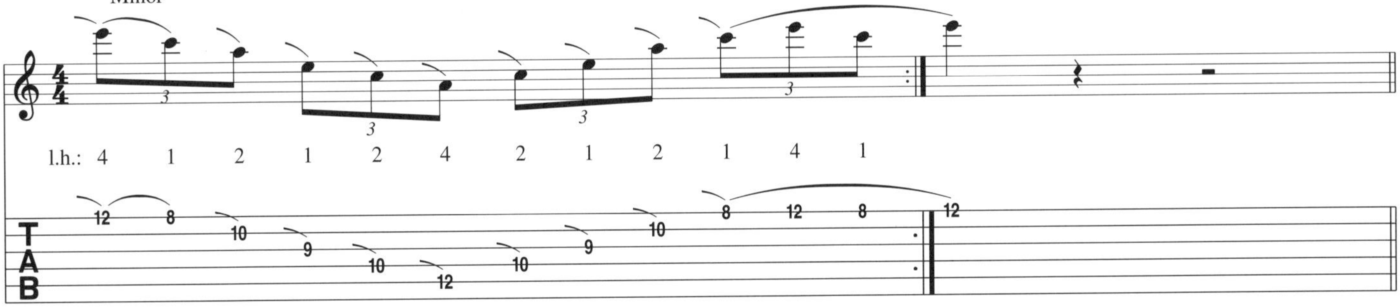

Example 195

Diminished

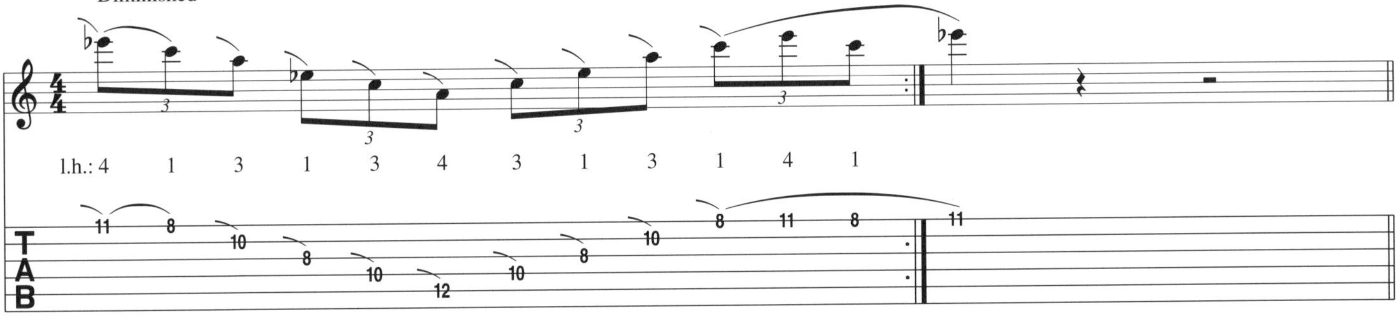

TAPPING

The basic technique of right hand tapping is a simple one. However, many guitarists fail to realize the importance of rhythmic accuracy or clarity of tones when using this technique. Practice each of the examples in this section with the metronome. Strive for clear, even tones.

Basic Sequences

The following examples utilize a one-string E minor arpeggio to illustrate various sequences that may be used in your improvisations.

16 Examples 196-206

Example 196

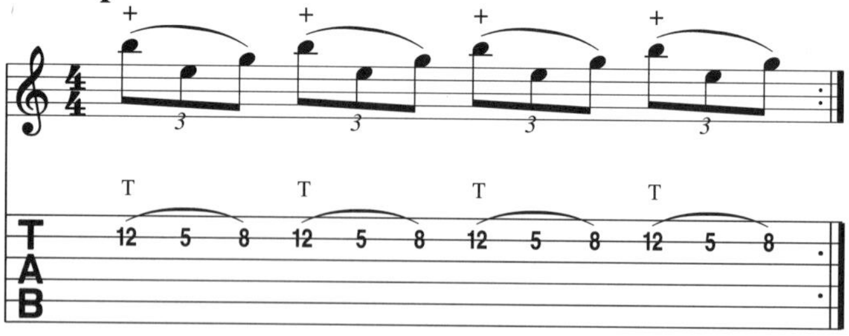

Example 197

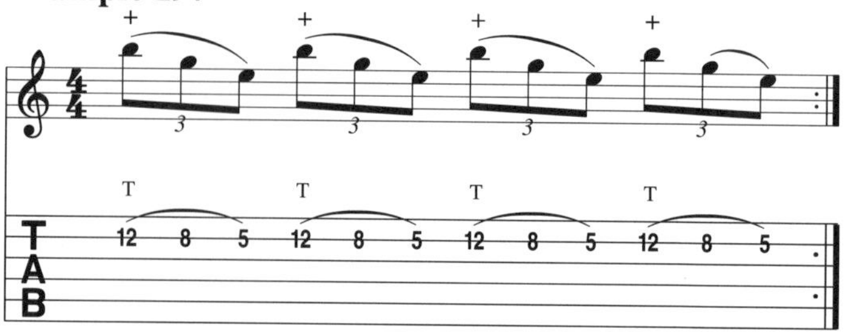

Example 198

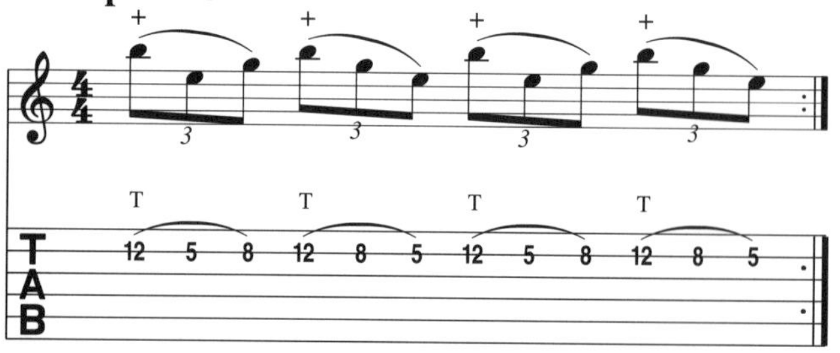

Example 199

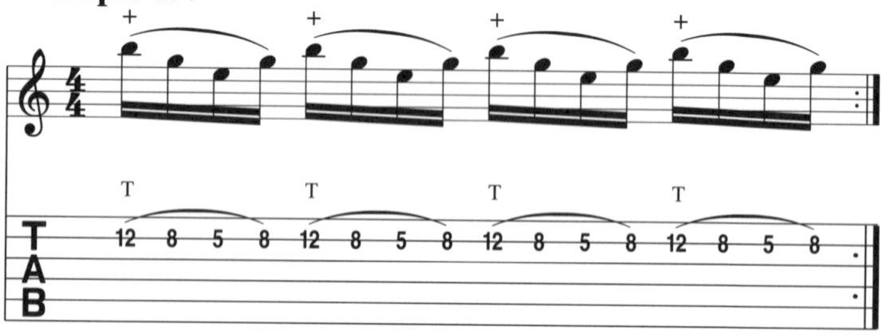

Example 200

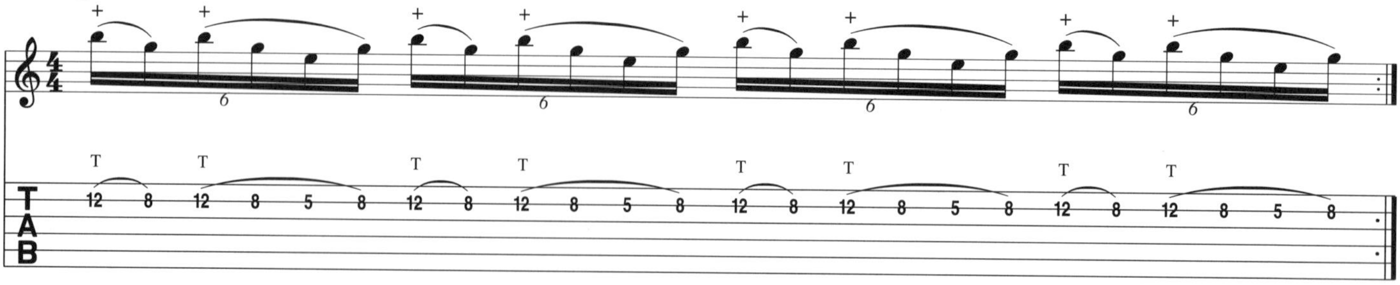

Next, we can incorporate an alternating high note, implying Em & C chords, respectively. By adding the C note on the third string, we create a Cmaj7 arpeggio.

Example 201

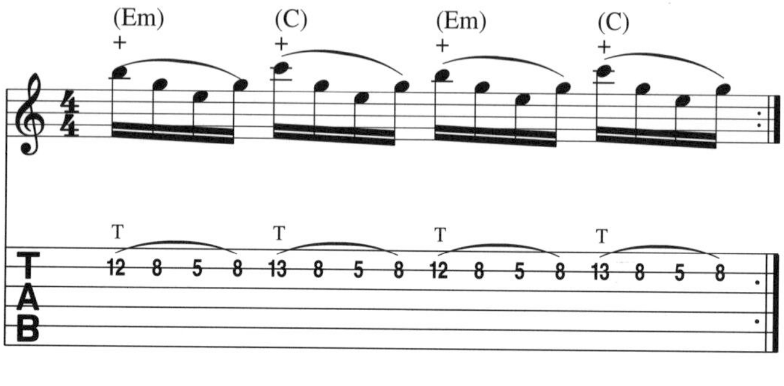

Example 202

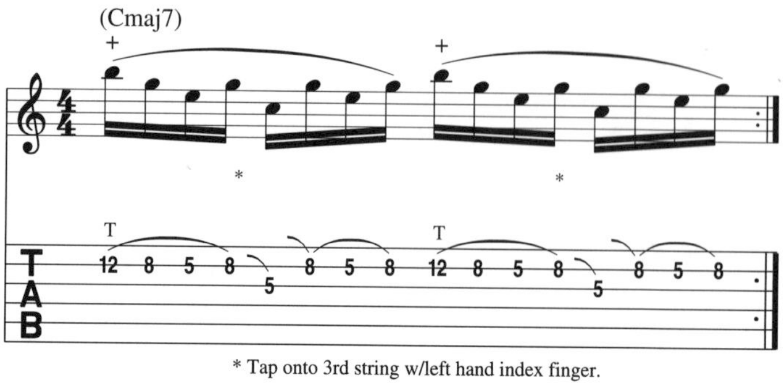

* Tap onto 3rd string w/left hand index finger.

Hero Of The Day
Metallica

* Guitar should be tuned 1/2 step down.

Intro.
```
|-----------------------------------------------------------------|
|-----------------------------------------------------------------|
|----------------2-------2-------2-------2-------4-----4-----4---|
|--------------2-------2-------2-------2-------6---4-----6-----6-|
|------0-----0-------2-------4-------5-------7-------7-----7-----|
|---2-----2-------------------------------------------------------|
```

```
|-----------------------------------------------------------------------
--|
|-----------------------------------------------------------------------
--|
|----------------2-------2-------2-------2---4---4-----4-----4---4p6p4-
--|
|--------------2-------2-------2-------2-----6-6---4-----6-----6-------
6\|
|------0-----0-------2-------4-------5-------7-------7-----7-----------
--|
|---2-----2-------------------------------------------------------------
--|
```

Verse.
```
|-----------------------------------------------------------------|
|-----------------------------------------------------------------|
|----------------2-------2-------2-------2-------4-----4-----4---|
|--------------2-------2-------2-------2-------6---4-----6-----6-|
|------0-----0-------2-------4-------5-------7-------7-----7-----|
|---2-----2-------------------------------------------------------|
```

```
|-----------------------------------------------------------------|
|-----------------------------------------------------------------|
|----------------2-------2-------2-------2-------4-----4---4-4-4-|
|--------------2-------2-------2-------2-------6---4-----6-6-6-6-|
|------0-----0-------2-------4-------5-------7-------7-----7-7-7-|
|---2-----2-------------------------------------------------------|
```

With distortion effect
```
|-----------------------------------------------------------------|
|-----------------------------------------------------------------|
```

Intro and mainriff.   (chords are F, Bb, G#, C#)

```
e------------------------------------------------------------]
h------------------------------------------------------------]
g------------------------3--3-------------------------6--6---]
D--3---3--3--------------3--3---6---6--6--------------6--6---]
A--3---3--3--x--x--x--x--1--1---6---6--6--x--x--x--x--4--4---]
E--1---1--1--x--x--x--x---------4---4--4--x--x--x--x---------]
```

Verses

```
e-----------1-----------------------------------]
h--1--------------------------------------------]
g-----------------------------------------------]
D-----------------------------------------------]
A-----------------------------------------------]
E-----------------------------------------------]
```

end of verses (play with distortion)

```
e-------1---------1---------1-------1--------1--]
h--1---------1---------1--------1-------1-------]
g-----------------------------------------------]
D-----------------------------------------------]
A-----------------------------------------------]
E-----------------------------------------------]
```

```
                 Hey!
e-----------------------------------------------]
h-----------------------------------------------]
g----------------3b-----------------------------]
D--3-----3--4---------3-----3--8--6-------------]
A--3--x--3--4---------3--x--3--8--6-------------]
E--1--x--1--2---------1--x--1--6--4-------------]
```

Solo:

```
e--------------------------------------------------------------------------]
h--------------------------------------------------------------------------]
g-------8----10-------8--8b--6--5---6-5------------------------------------]
D--10-------------6-----------------------8--6--8--8b--6--5----------------]
A--------------------------------------------------------------------------]
E--------------------------------------------------------------------------]
```

```
e-----------------------------------------------]
h-----------------------------------------------]
g-----------------------------------------------]
D---6---5---6---5---6---5---6>5--5>3------------]
A-----------------------------------------------]
E-----------------------------------------------]
```

Now, let's apply tapping to some scalar sequences. Notice that the right hand finger "follows" the scale under the left hand fingers.

Example 203

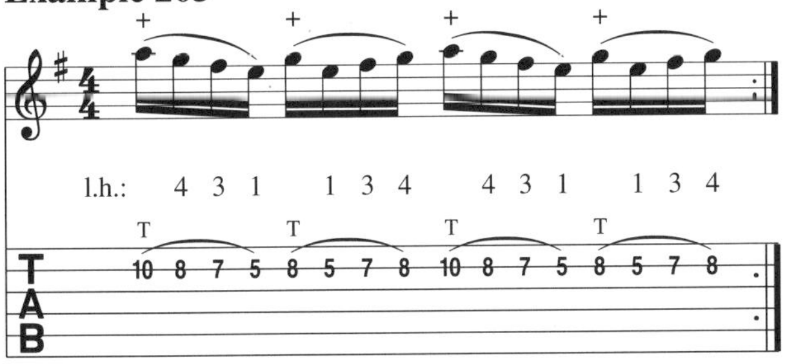

Example 204

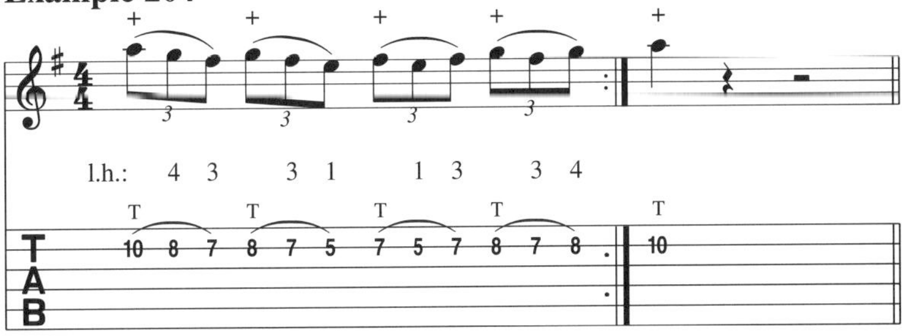

The same concept from the preceding examples may also be applied to diminished scale sequences. Take note of left hand fingering.

Example 205

Example 206

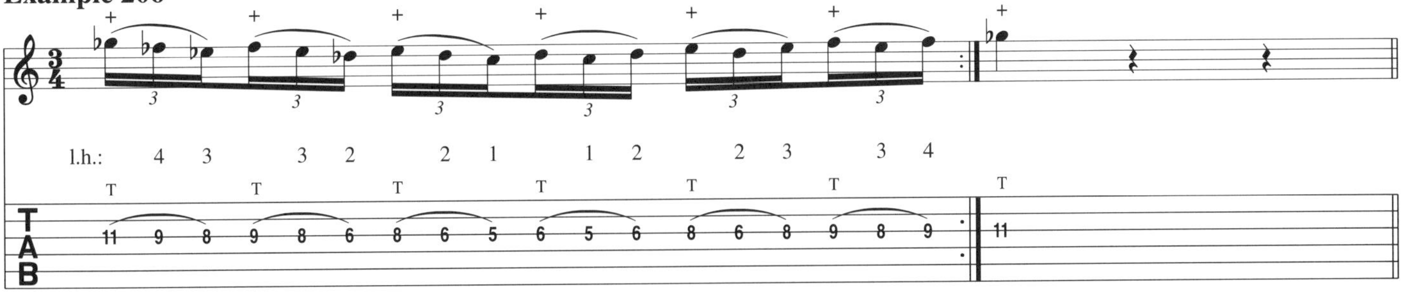

By combining some of these tapping techniques, we get a scalar passage in E major in a longer, positional application.

17 Example 207-208

Example 207

* Reach over behind left hand w/ right hand.

Studies

Now, let's put it all together. Below is a tapping study using a lengthy sequence of arpeggio and scale material. Take your time, have fun, and don't hurt yourself!

Example 208

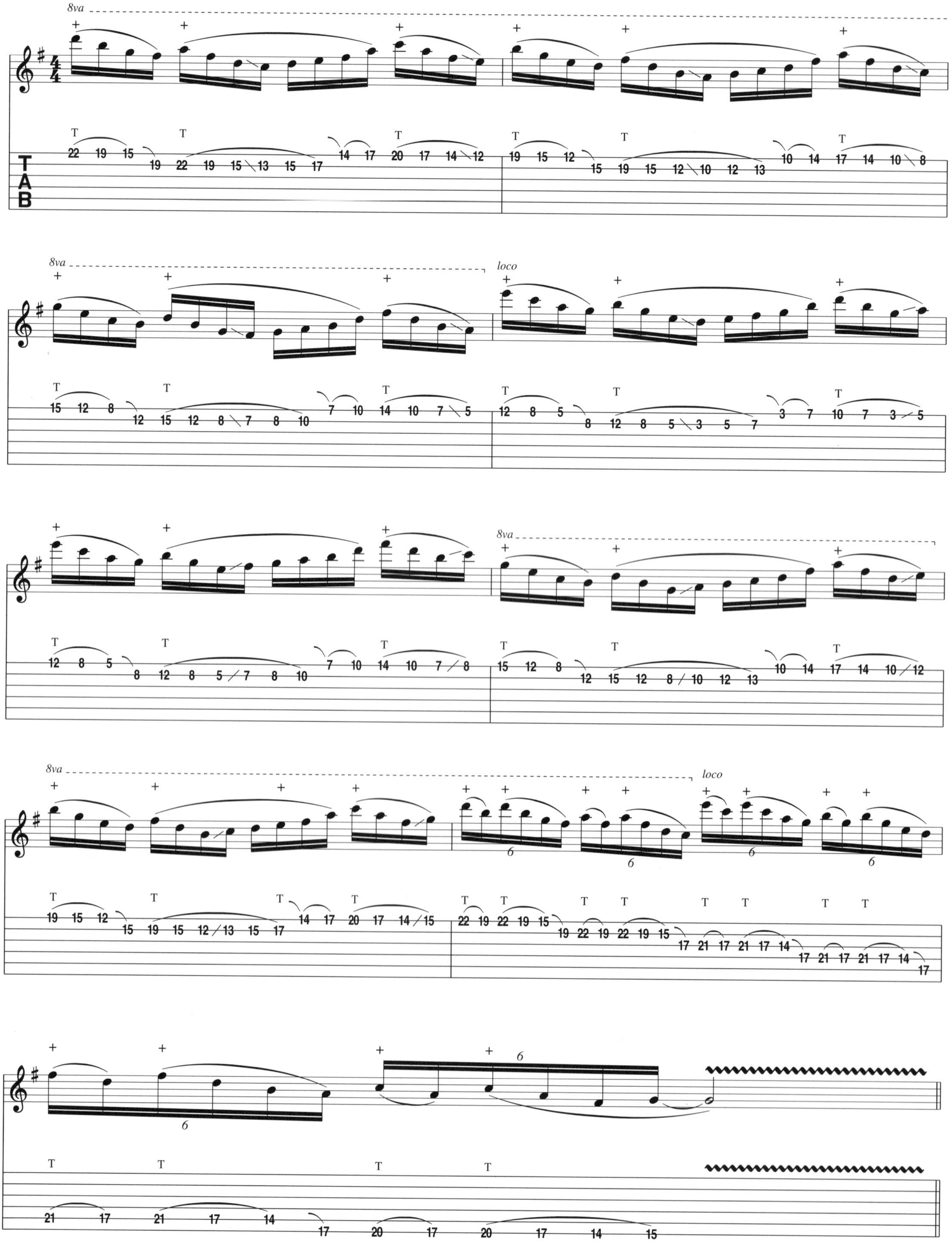

BENDING

Many guitarists have trouble achieving good intonation when bending strings. The following exercise incorporates bending into a line of scalar sequencing. Take care not to over-bend half-steps and under-bend whole-steps.

18 Example 209

Example 209

SCALE AND ARPEGGIO APPENDIX

The scale and arpeggio positions in this syllabus are shown for the purpose of reference and by no means represent a definitive list.

5 CAGED POSITION MAJOR SCALES

⦿ = Keynote

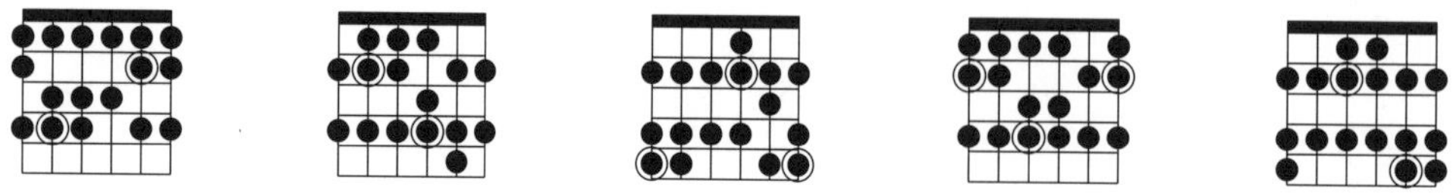

7 3-NOTE PER STRING MAJOR SCALES

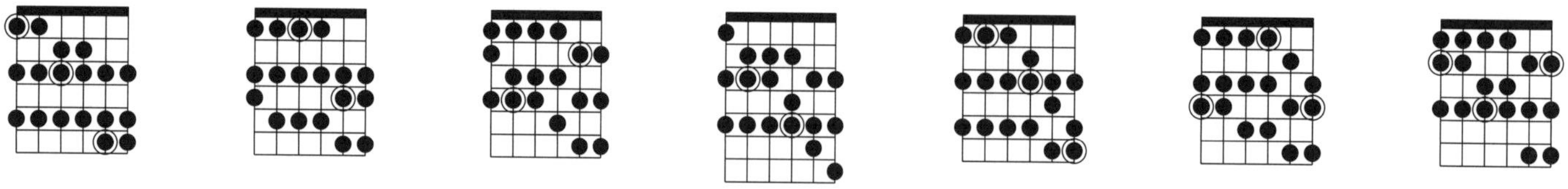

MAJOR ARPEGGIOS

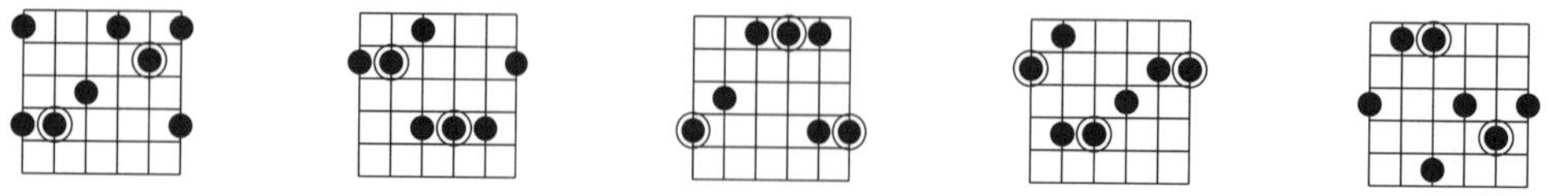

MINOR ARPEGGIOS

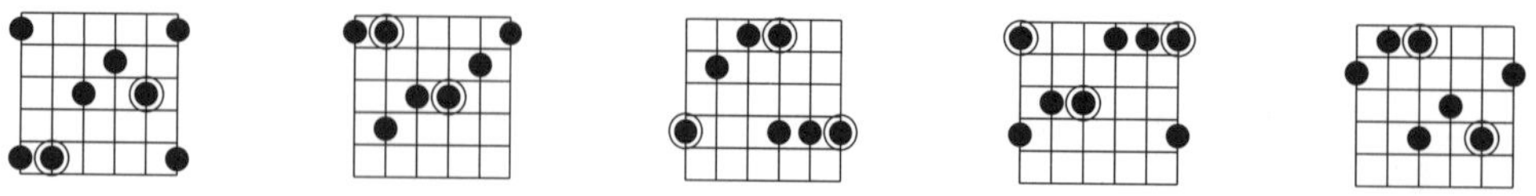

PENTATONIC SCALES

⦿ = Minor keynote ⊡ = Major keynote

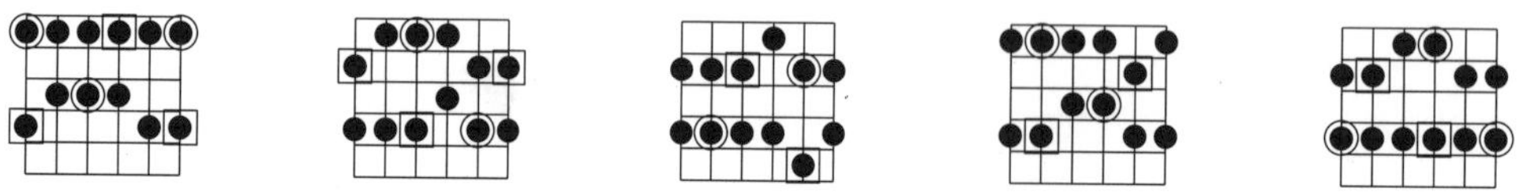